ARTHURIAN ROMANCES
Unrepresented in Malory's
"Morte d'Arthur"

Tristan and Iseult

Part II

AMS PRESS
NEW YORK

Reprinted from a copy in the collection of Brooklyn Public Library

Reprinted from the edition of 1899, London
First AMS EDITION published 1970
Manufactured in the United States of America

International Standard Book Number:
Complete set 0-404-00470-9
Volume three 0-404-00473-3

Library of Congress Number: 71-141784

AMS PRESS INC.
NEW YORK, N.Y. 10003

Here beginneth the treatise of the love-potion. How the Queen brewed it & gave it in charge to Brangoene & how Tristan & Iseult unknowing drank of it.

HE while that Tristan and his folk made them ready for the journey did the wise Queen Iseult, with much thought and care, prepare a love potion of such power and magic that did any two drink thereof they must needs, without will of their own, love each other above all things from that day forward ; death and life, sorrow and joy, were sealed within that little flask of crystal. Then the queen took the drink and spake softly to Brangœne: "Brangœne, my kinswoman, let not my words grieve thee : thou must go hence with my daughter, therefore hearken and heed what I say unto thee. Take thou this flask with the drink within it, and keep it in thy care. Treasure it above all thy treasures, see that none know of it, above all that none taste of it ; but when Iseult and King Mark be come together, then do thou pour out the drink as if it were wine, and see that the twain drink of it. Nor shalt thou share in it thyself, for 'tis a love potion, forget not that. I commend to thy

Of the brewing of the love potion, and the queen's charge to Brangœne care Iseult, my dearest daughter; my very life doth hang on her. She and I alike do I commend to thee on peril of thine eternal welfare—methinks I have said enough."

"My very true and dear lady," said Brangœne, "if this be the will of ye both, then will I gladly go with Iseult, and watch over her honour and her welfare as best I may."

Then Tristan and his folk departed with much joy for the haven of Whiteford, and for the love of Iseult, king and queen and all their household accompanied them thither. Weeping, her steadfast friends surrounded the princess; her father and mother filled the short space left to them with their lamentations; many eyes were red and tearful, and many hearts weighed down with sorrow for the loss of their life's delight, fair Iseult.

But the two Iseults, the sun and her rosy dawn, and the stately moon, fair Brangœne, when they three must part asunder, the one from the twain, then indeed was woe and wailing! Sad was the severance of such true companionship. Many a time and oft did the queen mother kiss them both.

Now they of Cornwall, and the men of Ireland the young queen's followers, were already aboard, and had taken their leave; Tristan was the last to enter the ship, leading by the hand the fair young Queen Iseult, the flower of Ireland; sad and sorrowful she went with him. Then the two bent in greeting towards the land, and prayed God's blessing be on it and on its folk. They pushed off from the shore, and with a loud voice one and all sang: "So sail we forth in the name of God." Thus they departed from Ireland.

By Tristan's counsel they set apart a private cabin for the queen and her maidens, wherein none might join them, save only at times Tristan, who now and again would go thither to comfort the young queen as she sat and wept, for she bemoaned herself sorely that she must thus perforce part from her land where she knew all the folk, and from the friends who were dear to her, and journey with an unknown folk to a land she knew not. Then Tristan would comfort her as he best could, and take her in his arms gently, even as a knight might his liege lady and the wife of his lord. But as often as he laid his arm around her, fair

Iseult would bethink her of her uncle's

death, and chide with him, saying: "Let
be, sir; take thine arm away, thou art a
weariful man; wherefore dost thou touch
me?"

"Do I then vex thee so sore, fair lady?"

"Yea, forsooth, since I hate thee."

"But wherefore, sweetest lady?"

"Thou didst slay mine uncle."

"For that have I made my peace."

"May be, yet I love thee not, for ere I
knew thee had I neither sorrow nor care:
thou alone with thy craft and courage
hast brought this sorrow upon me. What
brought thee from Cornwall to Ireland to
my hurt? They who brought me up from
my childhood, from them hast thou reft
me, and bearest me I know not whither!
What price hath been paid for me I know
not, nor what shall befall me."

"Nay, nay, fair Iseult, be at peace;
wouldst thou not rather be a rich queen
among strangers than poor and weak
among thine own kin? Honour and
wealth in a strange land, and shame in thy
father's kingdom, they weigh not equal, I
think me!"

"Yea, Sir Tristan," said the maiden,

"but say what thou wilt, I would have the lower lot with love and pleasure, rather than displeasure and trouble with great riches."

"Thou sayest true," answered Tristan; "but where one may have riches and pleasure alike, the two good things pass better together than either of the twain alone. But say, were it come to that that thou must needs have taken the seneschal for thine husband, what then? I wot well that would have made thee glad! Hast no thanks for me that I came to thine aid, and freed thee from him?"

"Too late," quoth the maid. "I might well have thanked thee then, when thou didst deliver me from him, but since then hast thou heaped such sorrow upon me that in sooth I had liever have wedded the seneschal than have sailed with thee! How worthless soever he may have been, had he dwelt but a short while with me then had he laid aside his evil ways, for this I know of a truth, that he loved me well."

Spake Tristan: "This tale seemeth me over-strange; 'twere great labour indeed for a man to act worthily against his nature. The world holds it for a lie that a worthless knight should do worthy deeds. Be content, fair lady; in a short while will I give thee for lord a king in whom thou shalt find henceforth virtue and honour, riches, joy, and fair living."

So they sailed onward with a favouring wind and a fair sea; but Iseult and her maidens were not wont to be exposed to the water and the wind, and ere long they were sorely in need of rest. Then Tristan bade them put to land for a little space, and as by good luck they came near a haven they ran the ship therein, and made it fast, and the more part of the folk went ashore to refresh themselves. But Iseult remained aboard, and Tristan went into the cabin to greet his liege lady, and sat him down beside her, and the twain spake of this thing and of that, till Tristan became thirsty and bade them bring whereof he might drink.

Now, beside the queen was there no one on board save little maidens, and one spied the flask where Brangœne had laid it, and said: "See, here is wine in this flask." But it was not wine that was therein, though like unto it, but bitter pain and enduring sorrow of heart, of which the twain at last lay dead. Yet the little maiden might know nought of this, so she took the flask from its hiding-place, and brought it to Tristan, and he gave forth-with of the drink to Iseult. She drank of it unwillingly enough, and after a space passed the cup to Tristan, and he too drank of it, and neither knew that it was other than wine. And even as it was done Brangœne entered, and saw well what had chanced. For very terror she became white as death. Cold at heart, she took that vessel of ill chance, and bearing it forth flung it into the wild and stormy sea. "Woe is me," she said within herself, "that ever I was born into this world! Miserable that I am, I have lost mine honour and failed in my trust. Would to God I had never come on this journey. I must ever bemoan that death took me not ere I pledged myself to sail with Iseult on this evil voyage. Alas, Tristan and Iseult, for this drink shall be your death!"

How Tristan and Iseult unknow-ing drank of the love potion

Now, when the man and the maid, Tristan and Iseult, had drunk of the potion Love, who never resteth but besetteth all hearts, crept softly into the hearts of the twain, and ere they were ware of it had she planted her banner of conquest therein, and brought them under her rule. They were one and undivided who but now were twain and at enmity. Gone was Iseult's hatred, no longer might there be strife between them, for Love, the great reconciler, had purified their hearts from all ill will, and so united them that each was clear as a mirror to the other. But one heart had they—her grief was his sadness, his sadness **Of the** her grief. Both were one in love and **begin-** sorrow, and yet both would hide it in **ning of** shame and doubt. She felt shame of her **their love** love, and the like did he. She doubted of his love, and he of hers. For though both their hearts were blindly bent to one will, yet was the chance and the beginning heavy to them, and both alike would hide their desire.

When Tristan felt the pangs of love, then he bethought him straightway of his faith and honour, and would fain have set himself free. "Nay," he said to himself, "let such things be, Tristan; guard thee well, lest others perceive thy thoughts." So would he turn his heart, fighting against his own will, and desiring against his own desire. He would and would not, and, a prisoner, struggled in his fetters. There was a strife within him, for ever as he looked on Iseult, and love stirred his heart and soul, then did honour draw him back. Yet he must needs follow Love, for his liege lady was she, and in sooth she wounded him more sorely than did his honour and faith to his uncle, though they strove hard for the mastery. For Love looked smiling upon his heart, and led heart and eyes captive; and yet if he saw her not, then was he even more sorrowful. Much he vexed himself, marvelling how he might escape, and saying to his heart: " Turn thee here or there, let thy desire be other, love and long elsewhere." Yet ever the more he looked into his heart the more he found that therein was nought but Love—and Iseult.

Even so was it with the maiden: she was as a bird that is snared with lime. When she knew the snare of love and saw that her heart was indeed taken therein, she strove with all her power to free herself, yet the more she struggled the faster was the hold Love laid upon her, and, unwilling, she must follow whither Love led. As with hands and feet she strove to free

herself, so were hands and feet even more
bound and fettered by the blinding sweetness
of the man and his love, and never half a
foot's length might she stir save that Love
were with her. Never a thought might
Iseult think save of Love and Tristan, yet
she fain would hide it. Heart and eyes
strove with each other; Love drew her
heart towards him, and shame drove her
eyes away. Thus Love and maiden shame
strove together till Iseult wearied of the
fruitless strife, and did as many have done
before her—vanquished, she yielded herself
body and soul to the man, and to
Love.

Shyly she looked on him, and he on her,
till heart and eyes had done their work.
And Tristan, too, was vanquished, since Love
would have it none otherwise. Knight
and maiden sought each other as often as
they might do so, and each found the other
fairer day by day. For such is the way of
Love, as it was of old, and is to day, and
shall be while the world endures, that lovers
please each other more as love within them
waxeth stronger, even as flowers and fruit
are fairer in their fulness than in their
beginning; and Love that beareth fruit

waxeth fairer day by day till the fulness of time be come.

> Love doth the loved one fairer make,
> So love a stronger life doth take.
> Love's eyes wax keener day by day,
> Else would love fade and pass away.

So the ship sailed gaily onwards, even though Love had thus turned two hearts aside, for she who turneth honey to gall, sweet to sour, and dew to flame, had laid her burden on Tristan and Iseult, and as they looked on each other their colour changed from white to red and from red to white, even as it pleased Love to paint them. Each knew the mind of the other, yet was their speech of other things.

In right maidenly wise Iseult questioned Tristan of his doings; they spake of how he came aforetime, wounded in a barque, to Dublin, how her mother had taken him in her care, and how Tristan had taught her Latin and the lute. And much she praised his valour when he slew the dragon, and she told how she had known him in the marsh for the minstrel Tantris, and later for Tristan. Then they spake together and Iseult said: "Ah, how was it that I thought better of my purpose, and slew thee not, that day? Had I known then what I know now, methinks it had been thy death."

"Wherefore," he said, "fair Iseult? What troubleth thee? what dost thou know?"

How Tristan and Iseult confessed their love to each other "What I know, that troubleth me; what I see doth bring me sorrow. Sky and sea weary me, life weigheth heavily on me."

She stirred a little, and leant against him, and the springs of her heart-sorrow rose to her lips and weighed down her head.

Then Tristan laid his arm around her gently, and spake softly: "Ah, fair and sweet, tell me what troubleth thee, of what dost thou make thy plaint?"

And Iseult spake, riddling: "*L'Amer*," she said, "doth trouble me, it weigheth down my soul, and bringeth me sorrow."

Then Tristan bethought himself of her words, and saw well how she spoke with a threefold meaning. *L'Amer* might alike mean love and bitterness, and the sea; and of the first would he say nothing, so he made answer:

"I ween, fair Iseult, that the sea and the wind troubleth thee; the sea, and the salt sea wind; thou dost taste them, and they are alike bitter to thee."

"Nay, nay, what sayest thou? I taste nor wind nor sea. *L'Amer* alone doth trouble me."

And Tristan whispered: "Of a sooth, sweetheart, so doth it me. *L'Amer* and thou, ye are my sorrow! Heart's lady, sweet Iseult, thou and the love of thee have turned my heart aside; so far have I wandered that nevermore may I find the right path. All that mine eyes behold is but weariness and sorrow, weakness of spirit and heaviness of heart; in all the world is there nought that my heart doth love save thee only."

Iseult spake: "Even so is it with me."

So the twain made their confession of love each to the other; he kissed her, and she him; and each drank of the sweetness that the heart may offer. Yet they kept the matter secret, that none in the world might know their hearts' desire. 'Twas enough that each knew the will of the other.

But the wise Brangœne, she watched

them in silence, and saw well what they would fain keep hid, and she thought within herself: "Alas! now see I well how love doth begin." And when she saw how day by day trouble of heart wrought upon them so that they grew pale and thin, a fear came upon her that this love might in truth be their death; and she said in her heart: "Now be of good courage, and learn what may be the truth of this."

So as they sat together one day she **How the** spake, saying: "Here is no man save we **twain** three alone, tell me, ye twain, what doth **gave their** ail ye? I see ye hour by hour sigh and **confi-** weep and make lamentation." **dence to**

Bran- "Lady," said Tristan, "an I dared I **gœne** would tell thee."

"Speak on, Sir Knight, tell what thou wilt."

"Nay, that may I not, saving that thou dost first swear an oath to be a friend to us, otherwise are we lost."

Then Brangœne sware an oath that she would truly and faithfully do their bidding.

"Dear lady," quoth Tristan, "have pity alike on me and on the princess: what hath chanced to us we know not, but a madness hath come upon us, we die of love! Aid us, we pray, for our life and death are in thine hands."

Then Brangœne spake to Iseult: "My princess, is it even as Sir Tristan saith?"

And Iseult answered: "Yea, friend of my heart."

Brangœne quoth: "Woe is us, for the devil hath made sport of us! Now see I well that I must deal for mine own sorrow and your shame; for so must it needs be if I would not let ye die. Yet hear my counsel: let this shame be kept secret between us three, it strikes at your honour, and if another know it ye are lost, and I with ye. Heart's mistress, sweet Iseult, thy life and thy death they rest with thyself alone. Have no fear of me, but do even as thou thyself shalt think best."

And that night Love, the physician, led Tristan to Iseult's side, and bound the twain together with such master skill and wondrous power that nevermore in all their lives might the bond between them be loosed.

So they sailed on their journey, blissful in each other's love, yet fearful lest any should espy their secret; and sad at heart when they thought how fair Iseult must needs be the bride of one whom she loved not. When they saw the coast of Cornwall, and all on board were joyous that their voyage was well-nigh ended, Tristan and Iseult were heavy at heart, for if they might have had their will never again would they have looked on land, but sailed the seas together for evermore.

How Iseult thought to deceive King Mark As they drew near to shore, Iseult bethought her of a ruse. She sought out Brangœne, and prayed her that she would, on the marriage night, take the place of the queen—for Brangœne was fair and a maiden, and Iseult had it in her heart to belong to none but to her lover Tristan. So she spake on this wise to Brangœne, who kept silence a space, and then answered:

"Dear lady, thy mother, my liege lady and queen, committed thee to my care; 'twas my part on this ill-fated voyage to have kept thee from this very sorrow. Through my carelessness have sorrow and shame come upon thee, so may I not complain if I must needs share the shame with thee, 'tis but right that I should take my part therein. Ah God! how came I to be thus forgetful?"

"Dear cousin," said Iseult, "wherefore reproach thyself? I know not of what thou speakest."

"Lady, 'twas but the other day I cast a crystal flask into the sea."

"'Tis true, but why should that so trouble thee?"

"Alas! that same flask, and the drink that was therein, 'twas the death of ye both!"

"How may that be? What is this wild tale?"

Then Brangœne told the twain the story, from beginning to end, even as it had chanced.

"Now in God's name," quoth Tristan, "were it death or life, the poison was sweet! I know not what may come of it, but such death it pleaseth me well! Shall fair Iseult indeed be my death, then would I die daily!"

And yet, however sweet love may be, a man must at whiles bethink him of his honour, and Tristan knew well that he owed both faith and honour to Mark, who had sent him to fetch his bride, and the twain fought hard with his love, and vexed heart and soul between them, yet was it of no avail, for since he had chosen Love, Honour and Faith alike must needs be put to the worse.

Then Tristan sent messengers in two boats to the land, to bear tidings of the coming of the fair Princess of Ireland; and Mark sent forth a thousand messengers through all the kingdom, to bid his knights How prepare a fitting welcome for their comrades, Iseult and the strangers who came with them, and landed in Mark himself received the twain even as Ireland a man welcomes that which he holds the dearest upon earth.

Then King Mark bade all his barons assemble at court within eighteen days, to witness his wedding with Iseult, and they came together, many a fair company of knights and ladies, all eager to behold fair Iseult, of whose beauty they had heard such tales. And when they had looked upon her, there was but one thought and one voice among them: "Iseult the fair is the marvel of all the world. 'Tis true what we have heard of her, she is even as the sun rejoiceth the hearts of men; never did any kingdom win so fair a maiden."

So King Mark and Iseult of Ireland were wedded, and the kingdoms of Cornwall and

England were laid in her hands, with the pledge that if she bare no heir to Mark, then should Tristan inherit them, and so was homage done to her.

When night fell, then were matters wrought even as Iseult had planned. When the queen put out the lights in the bridal chamber, then Brangœne, in the royal robes, lay down beside the king; but when the king asked for wine, that men were wont to drink on the bridal night, Brangœne arose, and when Tristan bare the lights and the wine, 'twas Iseult sat beside the couch. But the drink that she and Mark should have shared had been drunk long since, and the flask lay in the depths of the sea.

Herein is told how Queen Iseult would have slain Brangwene but repented herself & how Gandîn carried away the Queen & how Tristan rescued her

ow King Mark and all his folk, and the people of the land, loved and honoured Queen Iseult, for the grace and the courtesy that they found in her, and no man but spake her praises; and none knew how the matter stood betwixt her and Tristan, or thought evil of them. With that there came a thought into the queen's mind, since none but Brangœne knew aught of the deceit that she had practised toward King Mark, might it not be for her safety that she should live no longer? Were she no longer there, there would be little fear of any man discovering aught against the queen's honour. And if it were so that Brangœne had any love or friendship for King Mark, might it not be that she would reveal his shame unto him? And in this did the queen make clearly manifest that men fear shame and mockery more than they fear God, for she sent for two squires, strangers of England, and made them swear an oath, on peril of their lives, to do her bidding

Iseult fears lest Brangœne should betray her

without question. And when they had sworn she said: "Now mark well my mind: I will send a maiden with you, and ye three shall ride swiftly and secretly till ye be come to some wood, near or far, even as ye shall deem best, but apart from all dwelling-place of man. There shall ye smite off the maiden's head. And mark well all her words, and what she saith, that shall ye tell She lays me, and bring me back her tongue. And a plot be ye sure of this: if ye do my bidding well against on the morrow will I make ye knights, and Bran- give ye lands and riches so long as ye shall goene's life live." And all this did they swear to do.

Then Iseult took Brangœne aside, and said: "Brangœne, look at me well; am I not pale? I know not what aileth me, but mine head doth pain me sorely. Thou must go forth and seek me herbs and roots, and we must take counsel, else I fear for my life."

The faithful Brangœne answered: "Lady, thine illness grieveth me sore; let us not delay. But say, where may I find that which may do thee good?"

"See, here are two squires, ride with them, they will guide thee aright."

"Gladly will I go, lady."

Thus the three rode forth together, and they came to a wood, where was great plenty of herbs, roots, and grass, and Brangœne dismounted from her steed. Then the squires led her deeper into the wild woodland, and when they were far from all haunts of men the two seized the faithful maiden and threw her on the ground, and drew forth their swords to slay her.

Brangœne was so terrified she lay still on the ground, trembling in every limb. Fearful, she looked up to them : "Sirs, of your pity, what will ye do to me ?"

"Thou shalt die here !"

"Alas! wherefore? Tell me, I pray you."

And then one said : "What hast thou done to anger the queen ? She bade us slay thee, and it must needs be so. Iseult, our lady and thine, she hath commanded thy death."

Brangœne folded her hands, and spake, weeping : "Nay, sirs, for God's sake, of your mercy delay a while, and let me live till I have answered ye ; after that slay me if ye will. Know yourselves, and hereafter tell my lady the queen, that I have done nought to lose her favour, or that should bring her hurt, save perchance this one thing, and that I scarce believe it may be. When we twain sailed from Ireland we had each of us a garment white as snow, fairer and better than our other garments. When we were on the sea so great was the heat of Of Bran- the sun that the queen might not bear her goene's robes, but did on this white robe, and ware parable that only, and she ware it till it was soiled and stained and its whiteness marred. But I had hid my garment within my coffer, and its white folds were all unsullied. And when my lady came hither, and took my lord the king for her husband, on the bridal night would she wear her white robe, but 'twas no longer so fair as she would have it, so prayed she the loan of mine. Yet at first I forgot my duty and refused it to her, but at the last did I do even as she prayed. If it be not this that hath angered her, then I know not what it may be. God knoweth never at any time did I transgress her will and her command. Now do what ye will with me. Greet my lady from me as is fitting from a maiden to her mistress. May God in His goodness preserve her in life and in honour, and may my death be forgiven her. I commend my soul to God and my body to your will."

Then the squires looked pitifully the one on the other, they had compassion on the maiden and her bitter weeping, and repented them much that they had sworn to slay her, for they could find no fault in her, nor anything that was worthy of death. They took counsel together, and determined, happen what might to them, they would let her live. So they bound the maiden to a tree, high up, that the wolves might not touch her before they could come to her again, and took one of their hounds and slew it, and cut out its tongue, and rode thence. *The squires have pity on the maiden*

Then they told Queen Iseult how, with sorrow and pain, they had obeyed her commandment, and shewed her the tongue, and said it was that of the maiden. And Iseult said : " Now tell me, what did the maid say to ye ? "

Then they told her all from the beginning, even as Brangœne had told them, and forgat no word.

" Yea," quoth the queen, " said she no more ? " *Of Iseult's repentance*

" Nay, lady."

Then Iseult cried : " Alas for these tidings ! Wretched murderers, what have ye done ? Ye shall hang, both of ye ! "

"Lady," they said, "most gracious Queen Iseult, what dost thou say? Didst thou not beseech us, and lay pressure upon us, that we should slay her?"

"I know not what ye say of prayers. I gave my maiden into your care that ye should guard her on the road, that she might bring me back that which I desired. Ye must restore her to me or your lives are forfeit. Cowardly death-dealers, ye shall hang, both of ye, or be burnt on a pyre!"

"Nay," spake one of them, "lady, thy heart and thy mind, they are not pure and single, thy tongue is double indeed! But rather than lose our lives we will give thee thy maiden again, whole and in good health."

Then Iseult spake, weeping bitterly: "Lie to me no more: doth Brangœne live, or is she dead?"

"She liveth, gracious Iseult."

"Ah! then bring her back to me, and I will keep the promise I sware to ye."

"Lady, it shall be done."

Iseult bade one squire remain with her, the other rode thence to the spot where he left Brangœne, and brought the maiden

again to Iseult. And when she came into
the queen's presence Iseult clasped her in
her arms, and kissed her lips and her cheek
over and over again. To the squires she
gave for payment seventy marks of gold
on the promise that they should keep the
matter secret.

Now that Queen Iseult had tested *The*
Brangœne, and found that she was faithful *friend-*
and true, even to death, and that her *ship of*
courage was steadfast, even as gold tried in *Iseult and*
the furnace, the twain were henceforth so *Bran-*
one in heart and mind that nought could *gœne*
befall the one but it touched the other as
nearly. The court was full of Brangœne's
praise, all loved her, and she bore ill will to
no man. She was trusted alike by king
and queen, nought was done in the counsel-
chamber but Brangœne knew it. Also
would she serve Iseult and her lover
Tristan even as they might command her.
But this was done so secretly that no man
in the court had any suspicion. None
dreamed what were the thoughts and
words of Tristan and the queen.

And as the days passed on they learnt,
even among the folk around them, to speak
to each other by glances and hidden words,

as is the way of lovers. And as they grew
bolder even through their open speech
there ran a meaning, known but to themselves, love working in their speech, even
as a gold thread running through silken
tissue. None saw more in their words
than was fitting betwixt near of kin, for all
knew the love and confidence that were
betwixt Tristan and King Mark.

Yet even that love and confidence turned
to the king's undoing, for therewith did
Love ply her hidden game, and Mark held
their yea was yea, and their nay, nay; but
alas! 'twas far otherwise.

So they passed the hours gaily, sometimes glad, sometimes sad, as lovers are
wont to be. At whiles they were wroth
with each other, but without ill will; for
Of the so the way of Love—she kindleth anger in
way of the hearts of lovers, but the pain of anger
love is swiftly forgotten in the bliss of pardon,
when love is as it were new born, and
trust greater than it was before. Ye all
know well how anger ariseth and how
peace is made for but little cause, for lovers
are lightly prone to think that there is
another nearer and dearer than they, and a
small suspicion they make occasion for

great anger—out of a little grief they win a rich atonement. Thus did Tristan and Iseult, even as all lovers have done before them, and shall do while the world endures.

Now, Tristan loved all valiant deeds of knighthood, but when such might not be had he would spend his days in hunting and hawking, and often ride far afield—as it chanced even at this time.

For in these days a ship came to Mark's haven in Cornwall, and there landed from it a knight, a noble baron of Ireland, named Gandîn; he was rich, handsome, and courteous, so manly and strong of limb that all Ireland spake of his valour. *The coming of Gandîn*

Fairly clad, without shield or spear, he came riding to the king's court. On his back he bare a lute adorned with gold and precious stones, and strung as a lute should be.

He dismounted, and entered the palace, and greeted Mark and Iseult in fitting wise. Many a time and in many ways had he served the queen in her own land, through his knighthood, and the great love he bare her, and for her sake had he journeyed hither from Ireland.

Then Iseult knew him, and greeted him
courteously: "God save thee, Sir Gandîn."

"Gramercy, fair Iseult, fair, and fairer
than gold in the eyes of Gandîn!"

Iseult spake softly to the king, saying
who the knight was and whence he came;
and Mark hearkened, wondering much
why he bare a lute, and in sooth so did all
the folk, for such was not the wont of
wandering knights. Nevertheless would
Mark do him all the honour he might, both
for his own sake and for that of Iseult,
since he was the queen's countryman; so
he bade the stranger sit beside him, and
spake to him of his folk and land, and of
knightly deeds.

When the feast was ready, and water
was brought round to the guests to wash
their hands, then did the courtiers pray the
stranger to play the lute before them.
The king and queen said nought, they
would leave it to his own will; and when
he took no heed of their prayers, the
courtiers mocked him, calling him "The
Knight of the Lute," "The Prince with
the Penance"; and Gandîn said nought,
but sat beside King Mark, and ate and
drank, and heeded them not.

When the feast was over and the tables
borne away, then King Mark prayed him,
an he could, to pleasure them awhile with
his skill on the lute ; but Gandîn answered :
"Sire, I may not, save that I know what
my reward may be."

"Sir Knight, what meanest thou ? Dost **Gandîn**
thou desire aught of my possessions ? If **demands**
so, 'tis granted ; let us but hearken thy **a boon oï**
skill, and I will give thee whatever thou **Mark, who**
desirest." **promises**

"So be it," spake the knight of Ireland. **to give him**
Then he sang a lay which pleased them **whatever**
all well, so that the king desired him to **he may**
sing another. The traitor laughed in his **ask**
heart. "Tell me," he said, "what thou wilt,
that I may play even as shall please thee."

Now, when he had sung another lay
Gandîn arose and stood before the king,
holding the lute in his hand. "Sir King,"
he said, "bethink thee of what thou didst
promise me."

And Mark answered : "Of good will
will I do it. Tell me what wilt thou ?"

"Give me Iseult," quoth the knight. **He will**
"Friend," said Mark, "whatever else **have**
thou desirest thou shalt have, but this may **Iseult the**
not be." **queen**

"Verily, Sir King," said Gandîn, "I will neither much nor little, but Iseult alone."

The king spake : "Of a truth that shall not be !"

"Sire, wilt thou then break thy promise ? If thou be thus forsworn, henceforth shall men hold thee unworthy to be king of any land. Bid them read the right of kings, and if this be not so, then will I renounce my claim. Or dost thou, or any other, say that thou didst *not* swear to give me what I asked, then will I assert my right against thee, or against whomsoever the court may choose. My body shall be overcome with fight ere I renounce my claim. Choose thou a knight to ride in the ring against me, and I will prove by combat that fair Iseult is mine."

The king looked all about and on either side if he might find one who would dare to uphold his cause ; but there was no man who would set his life on such a wager, nor would Mark himself fight for his queen, for Gandîn was so strong and valiant that none durst take up his challenge.

Now, Tristan had ridden forth to the

woods to hunt, and as he came homeward to the court, he heard on the way the news of what had chanced. 'Twas all true; Gandîn had led the queen, weeping and lamenting bitterly, from the palace to the sea-shore. On the shore was pitched a tent, rich and costly, wherein he led the queen that they might wait till tide and river rose and floated the barque, which now lay high on the sand.

When Tristan had heard the tale from beginning to end, he mounted his horse and took his harp in his hand, and rode swiftly, even to the haven. There he turned aside, secretly, to a grove, made his horse fast to the bough of a tree, and with his harp in his hand took his way to the tent. The knight of Ireland sat there, armed, beside the weeping queen, whom he strove hard to comfort, but little might it avail, till she saw Tristan and his harp.

He greeted Gandîn, saying: "God save thee, fair minstrel!"

"Gramercy, gentle knight."

"Sir," he said, "I have hastened hither. Men have told me thou art come from Ireland; I too am from thence. I pray thee, of thine honour, take me back to mine own land."

Of Tris-tan's ruse The Irish knight made answer : " That will I do ; but sit thee down, play to me, and if thou canst comfort my lady, whom thou seest weeping so sorely, I will give thee the fairest garment that is in this tent."

" 'Tis a fair offer, Sir Knight," said Tristan. " I have good hope that I may do so ; an her grief be not so great that it will stay not for any man's playing she must needs be consoled."

Therewith he harped so sweetly that the notes crept into Iseult's heart and bare her thoughts so far hence that she ceased weeping, and thought but of her lover.

Now, when the lay was ended the water had come up to the barque, and it floated, so that they on board cried to the haven : " Sir, sir, come aboard ; if my lord Tristan comes whilst thou art yet ashore, we shall have but an ill time ! Folk and land alike are in his power—also he himself, so they say, is of such wondrous daring, so valiant and strong, he will lightly do thee a mis-chief."

This was unpleasing to Gandîn, and he

said angrily: "Now may Heaven hate me
if I stir hence a moment earlier for that!
Comrade, play me the lay of Dido, thou
dost harp so sweetly that I must needs love
thee for it. Now, play and banish my lady's
sorrow. Out of love for thee will I bear
thee hence with her and me, and will give
thee all I have promised thee, yea, and
more!"

"So be it," quoth Tristan.

The minstrel touched his harp again;
and he played so sweetly that Gandîn
listened eagerly, and Iseult was all intent
on the music. And when it had ended
the knight took the queen by the hand,
and would lead her aboard, but by now was
the tide so high, and running so strong,
that no man might reach the barque save
on horseback. "What shall we do now?"
asked Gandîn; "how may my lady come
aboard?"

"See, Sir Knight," quoth the minstrel,
"since I am sure thou wilt take me home
with thee, I think but little of what I have
here in Cornwall. I have a horse near by,
I ween he shall be tall enough to carry my
lady, thy friend, over to the barque without
the sea wetting her."

Gandîn said: "Good minstrel, haste, bring thy horse hither, and take also the robe I promised thee."

Tristan fetched his horse swiftly, and when he came back he swung his harp behind him, and cried: "Now, knight of Ireland, give me my lady, I will carry her before me through the water."

"Nay, minstrel, thou shalt not touch her; I will carry her myself."

"Nay, sir," said fair Iseult, "'tis needless to say he shall not touch me. Know of a truth I go not aboard save the minstrel bear me."

Then Gandîn led her to Tristan. "Comrade," he said, "have a care of her—carry her so gently that I shall be ever grateful to thee."

Now, as soon as Tristan held Iseult he spurred his steed forward, and when Gandîn saw it he spake in wrath: "Ha, fool, what dost thou?"

How Tristan won back Queen Iseult "Nay, nay, fool Gandîn," quoth Tristan, "'tis thou who art befooled; what thou didst steal from King Mark by thy lute, that do I bear away with my harp. Thou didst betray, now art thou betrayed. Tristan has followed thee till he has befooled thee! Friend thou hast indeed given me a rich garment, even the richest that thy tent did hold!"

With that Tristan rode his way, leaving Gandîn beyond measure sorrowful, his loss and his shame cut him to the heart; mourning he returned over-seas.

Tristan and Iseult rode homeward, rejoicing in their love; and when they came to the palace Tristan led the queen to King Mark, and spake bitterly: "Sire, God knoweth if thou dost hold thy queen so dear as thou sayest, 'tis a great folly to give her up lightly for mere lute or harp play! The world may well mock! Whoever saw a queen the chattel of a lay? Henceforth bethink thee, and guard my lady better!" *and reproached King Mark for his folly*

Here beginneth the tale
of King Mark's doubting
How Marjodo betrayed
the lovers & how King
Mark & Melot laid a
snare for them

I N these days had Tristan a companion, a noble knight, who held his lands from the king, and was chief seneschal at court; he was named Marjodo. The same bare Tristan love and honour for the sake of the queen, whom he loved secretly, though no man was ware of it.

Of Mar-jodo

The two knights had their lodging in common, and were fain to be of each other's company. It was the seneschal's custom to have his couch spread by Tristan's at night, that they might speak freely to each other, and he be solaced by Tristan's fair speech.

One night it chanced that the two had spoken long together ere Marjodo fell asleep, and when at length he slept soundly the lover Tristan arose softly, and stole secretly on the track that led to much sorrow for him and the queen. He thought himself unmarked as he trod the path that had often led him gladly to Iseult's side; snow had fallen, and the moon shone clear, but Tristan had no care to conceal his steps.

When he came to the queen's chamber Brangœne took a chess-board, and leant it against the light so that the chamber was darkened, and then she laid her down to sleep; how it chanced I know not, but she left the door undone, whereof came sorrow and trouble.

Now, as the seneschal Marjodo lay and slept, he dreamed that a fierce boar came out of the forest and ran into the palace, foaming, and gnashing his tusks, and oversetting all in his way, so that no man durst withstand him. Thus he came even to the king's chamber, and burst open the door and tare the couch to pieces, tossing it hither and thither; and Mark's men beheld, but none dare lay hands upon him.

With that the seneschal awoke, and would fain tell Tristan his dream; so he called on him by name, and when he answered not he called again, and felt with his hands, and knew the bed to be empty. Then he bethought him that Tristan was gone forth on some secret errand, not that he had any thought of his love for the queen, but he was somewhat vexed that, such friends as they were, Tristan had not told him his secret. So he arose and did on his garments, and stole forth softly, and looked around, and saw the track made by Tristan in the snow.

He followed the path through a little orchard, till he came to the door of the queen's chamber. There he stopped, trembling, for a strange doubt fell on him when he found the door undone. He stood awhile and gazed on Tristan's footprints, and thought now one thing, now another. One moment he deemed that Tristan had come hither for the love of one of the queen's maidens; and then again he deemed 'twas surely for love of the queen herself; so he wavered 'twixt one thought and another.

How he discovered the love of Tristan and the queen

At last he went forward softly, and found neither taper nor moonlight; a taper was burning, yet he saw but little of it for the chess-board that was set over against it. Yet he went forward still, feeling with his hands against the wall till he came near the queen's couch, and heard the lovers as they spake softly to each other.

Then was Marjodo sorrowful at heart, for he had ever loved and honoured Queen

Iseult, but now his love was overcome of anger. He hated and envied the twain, yet knew not what he might do in the matter. He bethought him of this and of that; he was so wrathful for the treachery that he fain had revealed it, but the thought of Tristan, and the dread of his anger should he do him a hurt, restrained him. So he turned him about, and went his way back, and laid him down again as one who had been sorely wronged.

In a short space Tristan came back softly, and laid him to bed again. He spake no word, nor did Marjodo, which was little his custom. From his silence Tristan misdoubted him, and bethought him to keep a better watch over his speech and actions; but 'twas too late, his secret was his no longer.

and be-
trayed
them to
the king
Then Marjodo spake secretly to the king, and told him how a rumour went about the court touching Tristan and the queen, that was but ill pleasing to the folk, and he counselled the king to look into the matter, and do as should best beseem him, for 'twas a thing that touched his wedded honour. But he told him not the true story as he himself knew it.

The simple-hearted king, who was himself true and faithful, was much amazed and heard him unwillingly, for the guiding star of his joy in Iseult would he not suffer lightly to be belied. Yet in his heart was he ill at ease, and could not but watch them secretly to see if he might find aught unfitting in their speech and bearing; yet could he find nought, for Tristan had warned Iseult of the seneschal's suspicions. *King Mark is loath te believe in Tristan's treachery*

Then the king bethought him of a ruse, and one evening when he was alone with the queen he spake on this wise : "Lady, I have a mind to go on a pilgrimage and may be long on the road; in whose care wilt thou that I leave thee?" *How the King would test Iseult*

"My lord," answered Iseult, "wherefore ask me? In whose care shouldst thou leave thy folk and thy land save in that of thy nephew Tristan? He is valiant and wise, and can guard them well."

This saying misliked the king, and he watched even more closely, and spake to the seneschal of his suspicions; and Marjodo answered :

"Of a truth, sire, 'tis as I say. Thou canst thyself see that they may not hide the love they bear to each other. 'Tis a great folly thus to suffer them. Much as thou dost love thy wife and thy nephew, thou shouldst not for thine honour endure this shame."

The matter vexed Mark much, for he could not but doubt his nephew, yet might he find no ground for his doubt.

Of Brangœne's wise counsels But Iseult was joyful, and told Brangœne, laughing and with much glee, of her lord's pilgrimage, and how he had asked her in whose care she would be left. Then Brangœne said: " My lady, lie not to me, but tell me truly,—whom didst thou choose ? " And Iseult told her all, even as it had chanced.

" Ah, foolish child ! " said Brangœne, " why didst thou say so ? Of a truth 'twas but a ruse, and the counsel was the seneschal's—herewith he thought to take thee. If the king speak to thee again on the matter, do as I shall tell thee, and answer thus and thus." So she counselled the queen.

When now king and queen were alone, Mark took Iseult in his arms, and kissed her many times on her eyes and on her lips, and spake : " Sweetest, I love nought beside thee, and now that I needs must leave, God knoweth it lieth heavy on my heart."

Then the queen said, sighing: " Alas and alas, my lord! I deemed thy speech was but in sport; now I see thou wert in very earnest." And she began to weep so bitterly that the simple king felt all his doubts vanish; he could have sworn that she spake from her heart (for in sooth women can weep without cause, and without meaning, so oft as it seemeth them good so to do).

Then, as Iseult still wept, Mark said: " Dearest, tell me what vexeth thee, why dost thou weep ? "

" Well may I weep, and much cause have I to lament. I am but a woman, and have but one body and soul, and both have I so given over to thee and to thy love that I can care for none beside. And know for a truth that thou dost not love me as thou sayest, or thou couldst not have the heart to journey hence, and leave me all alone in a strange land; by this I know thou lovest me not, and I must needs be sorrowful."

How Iseult misled the king

" But wherefore, fair Iseult ? thou hast folk and land in thine own power, they are thine even as they are mine, thou art mistress, and what thou dost command, that shall be done. And while I am on my journey shalt thou be in the care of one who can guard thee well, my nephew Tristan : he is wise and of good counsel, and will do all he may for thine honour and happiness. I trust him well ; thou art as dear to him as I may be, he will guard thee alike for thy sake and mine."

"Tristan !" said fair Iseult, "I were liever I were dead and buried than left in his care. He is but a flatterer who is ever at my side telling me how dear he holds me ! Yet I know well wherefore he doeth so : he slew my uncle and doth fear my hatred ! For that alone doth he ply me with flatteries, thinking to win my friendship, but it helpeth him little ! 'Tis true, I have spoken to him oft with lying lips and friendly glances, and laid myself out to please him, but I did it for thy sake, and lest men should bring against me the reproach that women aye hate their husband's friend. Ofttimes have I deceived him with my friendly words, so that he would have sworn they came from my heart ! Sir, leave me not in the care of thy

nephew Tristan, no, not for a day, if I
may persuade thee!"

Thus Iseult by her soft words soothed
Mark's heart, and laid his doubts to rest;
and he told the seneschal how that the
queen had contented him. But Marjodo
would not rest till he had persuaded the
king to test Iseult once more.

So on an even, as they sat in their How
chamber, Mark said: "My lady queen, Mark
since I must journey hence I would fain would try
see how a woman may rule a kingdom. the queen
All my friends and kinsmen who owe further
aught to me must needs treat thee with all
honour, but any who have not found favour
in thine eyes will I send out of the land, I
will no longer love those whom thou lovest
not. Otherwise live free and happy, and
do as shall best please thee. And since my
nephew Tristan displeaseth thee, I will
shortly send him hence, he shall return to
Parmenie, and see to his own land; 'tis
needful alike for him and the country."

"I thank thee, sire," said Iseult, "thou
dost speak well and truly. Since I know
now that thou art so swiftly displeased with
those who trouble me, it seemeth to me
that I should strive, in so far as I may, to

honour those who are pleasing in thine eyes. 'Tis neither my mind nor my counsel that thou shouldst banish thy nephew from court, so were I dishonoured, for all the folk would say that I had counselled thee to do it, in revenge for the death of mine uncle, and that were shame to me and small honour to thee. Also bethink thee well, who shall guard thy two kingdoms? Shall they be safe in a woman's hand? I know none who may guard them so well as thy nephew Tristan, he is thy nearest of kin, and shall be best obeyed. Should he be banished, and war come upon us, as may chance any day, and we be put to the worse, then would men reproach me, saying: 'If Tristan had been here, then should we not have had such ill success;' and all will blame me, so shall I forfeit alike my honour and thine. Sir, bethink thee better; either let me go with thee, or bid Tristan guard the kingdom; however my heart may be towards him, 'tis better he guard us than another shame us."

Now the king saw truly that Iseult's heart was set on Tristan's honour, and he fell again into doubt and anger. Iseult

also told Brangœne all that had passed, and
it vexed the wise maiden that she had
spoken thus, so she counselled her again as
to what she should say.   And when the
king held her in his arms and kissed her,
she said : " Sire, wast thou in very earnest *By Bran-*
when thou didst speak of sending Tristan *gœne's*
hence for my sake ?   If it were true, then *counsel*
his doubts
would I be grateful to thee, and in sooth I *are laid*
know I should trust thee, yet my mind *at rest*
misgave me that thou saidst it but to try
me ?   If I might know certainly that thou
dost hate all who are my foes, then should I
be assured of thy love for me.   Of a truth
had I thought thou wouldst hearken, I
should ere now have made my request to
thee to send thy nephew hence to his own
land, for I misdoubt me much, should evil
befall thee on thy journey, that he will
take from me the kingdom ; he has the
power to do so. If then thou wert in
earnest it might indeed be well to send him
to his own land, or to take him with thee
on thy journey ; and bid the seneschal
Marjodo guard me while thou art absent.
Or if thou wilt but let me journey with
thee, then mayest thou commit the
land to whomsoever thou wilt."   So she

caressed and flattered her lord till she had
driven all doubt from his soul, and he held
the queen for innocent, and the tale of her
love for Tristan a dream, and Marjodo
himself but a liar—yet had he spoken the
truth.

When Marjodo saw he could not bend
the king to his will, then he tried in other
wise. There was a dwarf at court, named
Melot of Aquitaine ; the tale went that he
was learned in hidden lore, and could read
the stars, but I will say nought of him
save what is writ in the book, and that
telleth nought save that he was clever,
cunning, and ready of speech. He was in
the king's confidence, and had free entrance
to the queen's apartments. With him Marjodo took counsel, and prayed him when he
was in the company of the women to take
close heed of Tristan and the queen, and if
he were so fortunate as to find sure proof of
the love betwixt them, then would he win
great reward from King Mark.

So Melot went his way, and dealt cunningly—early and late he watched the two,
till he saw well, by their sweet ways to
each other, that they were lovers. Then
he went his way to King Mark, and told

How Marjodo took counsel with Melot

him what he had seen, and the three,
Mark, Melot, and Marjodo, counselled
whether it were not better to forbid
Tristan the court.

Then the king prayed his nephew, on
his honour, to refrain from visiting the
queen's apartments, for he said tales went
about the court, and 'twere well he should
be careful, lest perchance slanders should
arise concerning him and the queen. From
henceforth Tristan avoided any place where
the queen and her maidens chanced to be
alone. But the courtiers were not slow to
note his altered bearing, and spake of him
in no friendly wise; so that his ears were
full of their chatter.

The time passed but sadly for the lovers. *Tristan*
They were sorrowful for Mark's suspicions, *and Iseult*
more sorrowful that they might no longer *wax sor-*
rowful for
meet and converse together as of yore. *their*
From day to day each began to lose heart *separa-*
and strength, and to wax pale and thin. *tion*
The one suffered for the other, Tristan for
Iseult, Iseult for Tristan. Nor was it
great marvel, for they had but one heart and
soul betwixt them; their sorrow, their joy,
their death and their life, they were inter-
woven the one with the other. The sorrow

of heart they bare in common was so manifest on their faces that few might doubt
their love who saw the whiteness of their
cheek.

When this had endured so long that
Mark knew surely they would seek to
meet did he but give them occasion thereto, he laid his plans warily, and commanded
that the huntsmen should make themselves
ready, and announced in the court that he
would ride forth hunting for the space of
twenty days, and that all who loved the
sport, or would ride with him for pastime,
should make them ready. Then he took
leave of the queen, and bade her do
according to her own pleasure, and be
joyful and glad at home; but secretly he
commanded the dwarf, Melot, to keep
watch upon Tristan and Iseult, and, if it
might be, aid their meetings. So he
departed to the wood with a great company.

But Tristan abode at home, saying to
his uncle that he was sick—in sooth he
thought to hunt other game! He and
Iseult cast about in their minds how they
might meet secretly, so that none should
know of it, but at first they could think of

How King Mark laid a snare for the twain

no way. Then Brangœne went to Tristan, for she knew well what ailed him, and they made great lamentation together.

"Ah, dear lady," he said, "canst thou find no counsel in this pass? For surely if we may not meet, 'twill be the death of Iseult and myself!"

"What counsel may I give?" quoth Brangœne. "Would to God we had never been born! We have all three lost our joy and our honour; never again shall we be free as of yore. Alas, Iseult! alas, Tristan! would that mine eyes had never seen ye, for all your sorrow is my doing! I know neither ease nor counsel whereby to aid ye, yet I know 'twill be your death and mine if this endure longer. See, since it may not better be, do this: take the twig of an olive, and cut it lengthwise, mark nothing thereon save on the one side a T and on the other an I. Then go thy way into the orchard. Thou knowest the little stream that floweth from the spring hard by the queen's chamber? Throw thy twig therein, and let it be carried past the chamber door,—there do we sit ofttimes and weep, the queen and I. When we see the twig float past, then shall we know

Brangœne devises a meeting

that thou art by the spring, beneath the olive-tree; there wait till Iseult may come to thee, my lady and thy beloved, and I with her, if it be thy will. The while I have to live am I thine and my lady's; might I but buy ye one hour of joy by a thousand hours of life, I would pledge all my days to lessen your sorrow!"

"I thank thee, fair lady," said Tristan. "I doubt me not of thy truth and honour, never were the twain more deeply planted in any heart. Should any good fortune chance to me, then should it turn to thy gladness."

With that he kissed her on the cheek. "Farewell, lady," he said: "do as shall seem best to thee, and commend me to my queen, fair Iseult, and bear us in thine heart."

"That will I, Sir Knight. But now would I go hence: do as I have counselled thee, and grieve not too sorely."

With that Brangœne departed, sad at heart.

Then Tristan did even as Brangœne bade him, and threw the twig into the streamlet, and he and his lady Iseult met by the spring and under the shadow of the

tree with such secrecy that they had met
eight times in eight days ere any was ware
of it.

But it chanced one night as Tristan
went thither that Melot spied him (I know
not how it so fell out) and crept after him.
And he saw him go to the tree; and ere he
had stood there long a lady came to him,
and he took her in his arms; but who the
lady might be, that could not Melot tell.

The next day, a little before noon, How
Melot came secretly to Tristan with false- Melot
hood on his lips, and said: "Alas, my sought to
lord! with peril have I come to thee, thou Tristan
art so beset with spies that I have had
much pain to steal hither, but my heart is
heavy for Iseult, the noble queen; she
sorrows sore for thee, and hath sent me to
thee since she would have none but me to
know of the matter. She greets thee, and
prays thee to come to her at the place
where thou didst meet her of late (I know
not where that may be), and at the same
hour at which thou art wont to come. I
know not of what she would warn thee;
but wouldst thou believe me, never did I
grieve for any one's sorrow as for thine, Sir
Tristan. An thou biddest me, I will take

what message thou wilt to her, but I dare
not stay with thee, for if the courtiers
knew mine errand harm would befall me.
They believe of a sooth that all that has
chanced 'twixt thee and the queen has
come about through me, yet was it none
of my counsel."

"Friend, thou dreamest!" quoth Tristan. "What fable wouldst thou tell me?
Are the courtiers mad? What have I and
my lady done? Out! to hell with thee!
Know in truth that an I did not think it
beneath mine honour to touch thee, thou
shouldst have no chance of telling thy
dreams in court henceforward!"

How Then Melot gat him swiftly to the
Mark and woodland to King Mark, and told him
Melot that he had at last found out the truth
laid in of the tryst by the spring. "Thou canst
wait for see the truth for thyself, sire, an thou wilt.
the lovers Ride with me at nightfall, 'tis the better
way; they will surely meet to-night, and
thou canst thyself see their doings."

So the king rode with Melot to await
his sorrow, and they came to the orchard
at nightfall, but they saw no place where
they might well hide themselves. Beside
the spring was an olive-tree none too high,

yet with spreading branches; thither they
betook themselves, and climbed into the
branches, and there they sat and held their
peace.

As it grew dark Tristan stole forth into
the orchard; he took his messenger in his
hand and dropped it where the waters
gushed forth, and saw it float away—'twas
token enough to Iseult that her lover was
at hand.   Then Tristan crossed the spring
where the shadow of the tree fell on the
grass, and stood there, awaiting her who
was his secret sorrow.

And as he stood there it chanced that Tristan
he spied the shadows of Mark and Melot, spies the
for the moon shone through the boughs so shadow
that he could well distinguish the shadows grass
of the two men; and a great terror fell
upon him, for he saw their ruse and his
danger.

"Ah God," he thought, "protect us!
If Iseult see not the shadows in time she
will come to me, and if she do 'twill be
sorrow and shame for us both.   Have us
in Thy keeping, guard Iseult's footsteps,
warn my queen betimes of the trap they
have laid for us, ere she speak or act so
that men think evil of her.   Have mercy

on us both, our life and our honour are in Thy hands to-night!"

Meanwhile Iseult the queen, and Brangœne, awaited his summons in the little garden where they had so oft bewailed their woe. They walked up and down, Iseult speaking ever of her love-sorrow. Then Brangœne saw the token floating in the stream, and signed to her lady, and Iseult took the twig and looked on it, and saw the T and I on either side. With that she took her mantle, and drew it over her head, and stole through grass and flowers to the olive-tree beside the spring.

How Iseult was warned of the snare set for them But when she came so nigh that each could see the other, Tristan stood still, which he was never wont to do, for never aforetime did she come towards him but he went to meet her.

Now, Iseult wondered much what this might mean, and her heart grew heavy within her. Timidly, with head bent down, she came towards him, fearing much for what she was doing. As she drew thus slowly nearer the tree, her eyes on the ground, she espied the shadow of three men, and knew there should be but one. With that she understood her danger, and

the meaning of Tristan's bearing towards
her.

"Ah, murderers!" she thought; "what
may this be? Wherefore this ambush?
I fear me my lord is hidden near at hand.
I see well we are betrayed. Blessed
Trinity shield us! Help us to depart
hence with honour, he and I!" Then
she thought again: "Doth Tristan know
this ill chance or not?" and again she felt
assured he knew it by his bearing.

Then she stood afar off and spake: "Sir   How
Tristan, it grieveth me much that thou   Iseult re-
shouldst so count on my simplicity as to   proached
deem I would come and speak with thee   Tristan
here! That thou shouldst guard well
thine honour as against thine uncle and
myself, that indeed would befit thee well,
and would better accord with thy faith and
my honour than to pray of me so late and
so secret a meeting! Now say, what
wouldst thou? I came here with fear
and trembling, for Brangœne would not
have it otherwise. When she left thee
to-day she prayed and counselled me to
come hither and hear thy plaint; yet have
I done wrong in that I have followed her
counsel. 'Tis true that she sitteth near at

hand, yet, though I know myself to be
safe, for fear of evil tongues I would give
one of my fingers from off my hand ere
any should know that I have met thee
here. Folk have told such tales of us
twain! They sware that we were sick
and sorrowful by reason of our treasonable
love to each other! The court is full of
such fables. God knoweth how my heart
standeth toward thee. I will say no more
save that I speak the truth of my feeling
toward thee, and that God is my witness
I never gave my heart to any man, heretofore, or to-day, save to him to whom I
gave the first blossom of my maidenhood.
My lord King Mark doeth ill to suspect
me for thy sake, Sir Tristan, for he himself
well knoweth my mind toward thee. They
who whisper such tales of us in his ear are
but evil counsellors. A hundred thousand
times have I shewn thee a friendly bearing
through the love I bear to him whom I
ought to love,—never for falsehood!
Whether he were knight or squire, 'twas
but right I should shew kindness to one
who was my lord's kinsman. Now men
will turn that to my hurt! Yet will I
not hate thee for their lies. Sir Knight,

what thou wouldst say to me, that say,
and let me go hence ; I may not stay here
longer."

"Dearest lady," spake Tristan, "no How
doubt had I as to thy feelings towards me. Tristan
I knew well thou wouldst do as befitted answered
thine honour. Give no ear to the liars who to her
have slandered thee and me, and brought speech
us, innocent, out of our lord's favour ;
God reward them ! My lady queen, I
pray thee counsel my lord that the wrath
and rancour he beareth against me be
hidden, and that he be courteous to me for
but eight days more—till now have ye both
borne yourselves as if ye loved me—so will
I within that time make ready to depart
hence. We shall be dishonoured, the
king, thou, and I alike, if ye bear yourselves thus towards me ere I depart, for all
men will say : 'Of a truth was there somewhat in that tale. Mark ye how Sir
Tristan has fallen out of the king's favour,
and is departed hence ?'"

"Sir Tristan," said Iseult, "I would
rather die than that I should pray my lord
to do aught against thee for my sake.
Thou knowest well that because of thee he
has this long while past been ill disposed

towards me; did he know that I had met thee here, alone and by night, henceforth would he shew me neither love nor honour. If things may so chance, alas! I know not. But I wonder much how my lord came thus to suspect me? I know not who hath slandered us, but matters stand ill enough for us both. May God look upon the thing and better it. Now, Sir Knight, give me leave, I must go hence; do thou, too, depart. Much do I grieve for thy sorrow and trouble; I had much against thee, yet will I not count it to thy wrong that I should hate thee; sorry enough am I that thou shouldst thus be troubled for no cause. I will think the matter over; and, Sir Knight, when the day comes that I must go hence, then may the Queen of Heaven have thee in her keeping. If I thought there were any power in my prayers or my counsel, then would I do all I might for thee, though it should bring me ill. Yet, since thou hast thought no treason against me and my lord, will I do thy bidding as best I may."

"I thank thee, lady," said Tristan; "if thou winnest favour or not I pray thee let me know straightway. But if I hear nought, and must needs go hence without delaying, so that I see thee not again, whatever be my lot, gracious queen, thou must needs be blessed, for a truer lady never trod this earth. My queen, I commend thy soul and body, thine honour and thy life, to the care of God."

Thus they parted. The queen went her way, sighing and lamenting, sorrowing secretly in heart and soul. Tristan also departed, sad and weeping. But King Mark who sat up in the tree grieved even more. It went to his heart to think that he had so sorely wronged his nephew and his wife, and a thousand times with heart and lips he cursed those who had brought him to this pass. Bitterly he reproached the dwarf Melot for having deceived him and slandered the innocent queen. They descended from the tree, and rode back to the hunt heavy at heart—Melot, that he had ever meddled in the matter, and Mark for the suspicion which had wronged his nephew and his wife, and his own self yet more, and which had caused such ill talk in the land.

How King Mark bethought him he had wronged his queen and Sir Tristan

Herein ye may read of
the testing of Queen
Iseult & how she brav-
-ed the ordeal of the
red-hot iron

N the morning the king bade the rest of his company continue the hunt, but he himself returned to the court, where he sought Iseult. "Say, lady queen, how hast thou passed the time in mine absence?"

"Sire, my idleness was undeserved sorrow; my labour, harp and lyre."

"Undeserved sorrow?" quoth Mark. "What was that, and how did it chance?"

Iseult smiled a little. "However it chanced, it chanced and doth chance to-day and every day. Sorrow and vain reproaches are my lot and that of all women, therewith cleanse we our hearts and enlighten our eyes. Yet ofttimes do we make a great sorrow of nought, and forget it as quickly." Thus she mocked him.

But the king marked her words and said: "Now, lady, tell me, does any one here, or dost thou, know how matters are with Tristan? They told me he was sick when I departed."

"'Twas true, sire."

"How dost thou know? Who told thee?"

"I know nought, save that Brangœne spake to me of his sickness a while back. She saw him yesterday, and prayed me that I would make his plaint to thee, and pray thee not to think aught against his honour, but hide thy displeasure for these eight days longer, when he will make him ready so that he may leave thy court and thy land in all honour. That he prayed of us both."

So she told him all Tristan's will even as he had spoken it by the spring, and as Mark himself had overheard.

But the king said : "My lady queen, ill luck may he have who caused me to think ill of Tristan ; I repent me sore of it, for in these last days have I learnt his innocence, and my ill will is at an end. Dear lady, by the love thou dost bear to me I pray thee to lay aside thine anger, do as thou wilt, but make peace betwixt me and him."

"Nay, to what good, my lord?" said the queen, "for even if thou dost lay aside thy suspicion, to-day, to-morrow wilt thou take it to thine heart again."

"Nay, of a truth, lady, never more. I

will never again think aught against his honour and thine, my queen. Show favour to him if thou wilt." Thus he swore to her.

Herewith Tristan was sent for, and the suspicion laid to rest between them. Iseult was commended to Tristan's care, that henceforth he should be the keeper of the queen's chamber.

So for a while Tristan and his lady Iseult led a happy life; their joy was full, their desire was granted them after much sorrow. But not for long might it endure, for do as they might Tristan and Iseult might not guard themselves so well but that the king should find fresh matter for suspicion. Again Mark knew not what to think: he suspected both, yet would suspect neither; he thought them true, yet deemed they lied to him; he would not have them guilty, yet would not speak them free of guilt. This was a heavy load on the heart of the doubter.

At last he bethought him he would call his lords together, and take counsel on the matter; so he summoned all those in whom he might trust, and laid all his trouble bare to them telling them of the tale which went

Of the love of Tristan and Iseult and how King Mark once more misdoubted him of their truth

about the court, and which so nearly touched his honour, and how, do what he might, he could not lay his doubts to rest. But now was the tale so spread abroad in the land that it seemed to him alike for his sake and the queen's 'twas time that her innocence should be made clear in the sight of all men. He besought their counsel as to how the matter should be cleared up.

How the king besought counsel of his lords

Then the lords, his friends, bade him assemble a great council at London, in England, and there make known to all the bishops, who knew well the law of the church, the doubt and sorrow in which he found himself. The council was therefore summoned without delay to meet at London, after Pentecost, on the last days of May. Of priests and lay folk a great number came together by the king's command, and thereto came King Mark and Iseult his queen, heavy at heart, and in much fear and trembling: Iseult feared greatly lest she lose her life and her good fame, and Mark also feared lest his gladness and his honour be shamed through his wife Iseult.

Then Mark sat at the council, and laid bare to all the princes of his land how he was troubled and perplexed by this tale or

scandal, and prayed them earnestly for
God's sake that they would bethink
them of some means by which the matter
might be fairly judged, and, for good or for
ill, an end put to it. And some said one
thing and some another, till many men had
spoken their minds.

Then there stood up one of the princes,
who by his age and wisdom was well fitted
to give good counsel; a man noble and
ancient, grey-haired and wise, the Bishop of
Thames. He leaned on his staff and spake:
"My lord king, hear me. Thou hast
called us princes of England together that
we may aid thee by our counsel as thou hast
need. Sire, I am one of these princes, and
well advanced in age; I think I may well
take upon me to speak my mind in the
matter; if thou thinkest my counsel good
thou canst follow it. My lady the queen
and Sir Tristan are suspected by many of
having betrayed thee, yet can nought be
proved against them—so do I understand
the matter. How then mayst thou pass
judgment on thy nephew and thy wife, since
none have found them offending? No man
can accuse Tristan of it but he is ready with
an answer to the charge; even so is it with

The
Bishop of
Thames
gives the
king
counsel

the queen. Thou canst prove nought. But since the court holdeth them so strongly in suspicion, I counsel thee that thou forbid the queen thy bed and thy board till the day that she can shew herself free of offence against thee and against the land. The tale is spread abroad, and men speak of it daily, for alas! to such scandals, be they true or false, men's ears are ever wont to be open, and whatever evil be in the story, of that will they make the worst. But whether true or false the mischief and the scandal are so widespread they must needs injure thee and be held amiss by the court. Therefore I counsel thee to call the queen hither that all present may hear her answer to the charge, and see if she be ready to give open proof of her innocence."

This counsel seemed good to King Mark, and he bade them summon Queen Iseult, and she came to the council-chamber. When she was seated the grey-haired Bishop of Thames arose, and spake as the king bade him:

"Lady Iseult, gracious queen, be not wrathful at my speech; the king my master hath bid me speak, and I must needs obey him. God is my witness, I would fain say nought that could reflect on The bishop declares the king's will to Queen Iseult thine honour and on thy fair fame. My lady queen, thy lord and husband hath bid me speak to thee of a charge openly brought against thee. I know not, nor may he know, how it hath come about, he knoweth only that court and country alike couple thy name with that of the king's nephew, Sir Tristan. I pray God, my lady queen, that thou art innocent of this sin—yet doth the king doubt; the court is so full of the rumour. My lord himself hath found in thee nought but good; 'tis not his thought but the talk of the court that hath brought this suspicion upon thee. Therefore doth he call thee hither that his friends and councillors may hear thee, if perchance by their aid an end may be put to this slander. Now methinks it were well that thou shouldst make answer to the king in this matter, here, in presence of us all."

Then Iseult, the quick-witted queen, seeing that it fell to her to speak, arose and answered: "My king, my lord bishop, Queen Iseult's answer lords of the land and all ye courtiers, ye shall all know well that I deny my lord's shame and mine, and I shall deny it both now and at all times. Ye lords all, I know well that this accusation hath been brought against me, it is now over a year, both at court and abroad ; yet ye yourselves know that no man may be so fortunate that, however well he may live, evil shall never be spoken of him. Therefore I marvel not if such chance should also befall me. I may never be left in peace, I must ever be slandered and misjudged since I am here a stranger, and have neither friend nor kinsfolk in the land—there are but few here whom my shame may touch. Ye all and each, whether rich or poor, believe readily in my misdoing ! If I knew now what I might do, or what counsel I might follow whereby I might prove mine innocence, and win again your favour and my lord's honour, I would readily agree to it. What would ye have me do ? Whatever judgment may be passed upon me thereto will I readily submit, that your suspicions may be laid to rest, yet even more that mine honour and that of my lord may be maintained."

Then the king spake: "My lady queen, hereby shall the matter be set at rest. If I may pass judgment upon thee as thou hast prayed us to do, thus shalt thou give us certainty : submit to the ordeal by red-hot iron, as we here counsel thee ! "

This the queen did ; she sware to undergo the ordeal even as they should ordain, six weeks hence, in the town of Cærleon.

Iseult promises to submit to the ordeal by red-hot iron

Thus the king and the lords departed from the council.

Iseult remained alone, sorrowful and sore dismayed at heart, for much she feared that her unfaithfulness must now be made manifest, and she knew not what to do. So with prayer and fasting she made supplication to Heaven to aid her. And a thought came into her mind. She wrote a letter to Tristan, bidding him be at Cærleon early on the morn of the day she must arrive there and await her on the shore. And this Tristan did, journeying thither in pilgrim's guise, his face stained and soiled, and his appearance changed.

Now, Mark and Iseult came thither by water, and as they drew to shore the queen saw Tristan and knew him. As the ship cast anchor in the stream Iseult commanded they should ask the pilgrim if he were strong enough to carry her to shore, for on

Of the queen's ruse

that day she would have no knight to bear her.

Then all the folk cried: "Come hither, thou holy man, bear our lady the queen to land."

Tristan came at their call, and took the queen in his arms and bore here to the shore; and as he held her Iseult whispered in his ear that as he set foot on land he should fall with her. And this he did; as he stepped out of the water on to the shore the pilgrim sank down on the earth as if he could not help himself, so that the queen fell from his clasp and lay beside him on the ground.

Then the folk came swiftly with sticks and staves, and would do the pilgrim an harm. "Nay, nay, let be," cried Iseult, "the pilgrim could not help himself, he is sick and feeble, and fell against his will."

Then they all praised her much that she was not wrathful with the pilgrim, but Iseult spake, smiling a little: "Were it then so great a wonder if the pilgrim had thought to mock me?" And as Mark stood near and harkened, she spake further: "Now I know not what shall befall me, for ye have all seen well that I may not swear that no man save the king ever held me in his arms or lay at my side!"

Thus they rode gaily, jesting the while of the palmer, till they came into Cærleon. There were many nobles, priests, and knights, and of lesser folk a great crowd. Bishops and prelates were there, ready to do their office and bless the ordeal. They had all things in readiness, and the iron was brought forth.

The good Queen Iseult had given in charity her silks and her gold, her jewels and all she had, horses and raiment, praying that Heaven would look favourably on her, forgive her what she had done amiss, and preserve her honour. Herewith she came to the Minster with good courage to face her ordeal.

She wore next her skin a rough garment of hair; above it a short gown of woollen stuff, a hand's breadth above her ankles; her sleeves were rolled up to her elbows, and her hands and feet bare. Many hearts and many eyes beheld her with pity.

Herewith they brought forth the relics, and bade Iseult swear her innocence of this sin before God and the world. Now had Iseult committed life and honour to Heaven, so hand and heart did she proffer reverently to the relics and the oath.

Now were there many there who would fain from ill will have had the queen's oath turned to her shame and downfall. The envious seneschal, Marjodo, strove to harm her in every way he might; while there were many who honoured Iseult, and would fain see her come off scatheless; so there was great strife among them as to the manner of the queen's oath.

"My lord the king," spake Iseult, "whatever any may say, I must needs swear in such wise as shall content thee. Say thyself what I shall speak or do. All this talk is too much. Hearken how I will swear to thee. No man hath touched this my body, hath held me in his arms, or lain beside me other than thou thyself, and this man whom I cannot deny, since ye all saw me in his arms—the poor pilgrim! So help me God and all the saints, to the happy issue of this ordeal! If this be not enough, my lord, I will better mine oath as thou shalt bid me!"

"Lady," said King Mark, "methinks 'tis enough. Now take the iron in thine hand, and God help thee in thy need."

"Amen," said fair Iseult. Then in God's name she seized the iron, and carried it, and it burnt her not.

And so, had men but known it, they might have seen that God at whiles doth let the wrong triumph, since He turned not this oath, which was true in the letter yet false in spirit, to the confusion of the queen, but ruled matters so that she came forth from the ordeal victorious, and was held in greater love and honour by Mark and his people than ever before ; all his thoughts and all his heart were truly set upon her, and his doubts had passed away.

The story turneth to Tristram: How he abode with Duke Gilân & slew the giant Urgan & won the dog Petit-Crû

ow Tristan when he had borne Iseult to the shore at Cærleon departed secretly from England, and came to Wales, to the court of Duke Gilân. He was a noble prince, unmarried, young and rich, free, and light of heart. There was Tristan a welcome guest, for Gilân had heard great marvels of his valiant and knightly deeds, and did all in his power to honour him and give him pleasure; but Tristan was ever sorrowful, plunged in thought over his ill fortune.

One day it chanced that Tristan sat by Gilân, sad, in deep thought, and sighing often; his host noticed this, and bade men bring him his little dog, Petit-criu, his heart's delight and the joy of his eyes, that erewhile came to him from Avalon. As he bade, so was it done: a rich purple cloth was laid upon the table, and the dog placed upon it. 'Twas a fairy dog, as I have heard tell, and had been sent to the duke from the land of Avalon, as love token, by a fay.

The dog Petit-criu   No tongue could tell the marvel of it; 'twas of such wondrous fashion that no man might say of what colour it was. If one looked on the breast, and saw nought else, one had said 'twas white as snow, yet its thighs were greener than clover, and its sides, one red as scarlet, the other more yellow than saffron. Its under parts were even as azure, while above 'twas mingled, so that no one colour might be distinguished; 'twas neither green nor red, white nor black, yellow nor blue, and yet was there somewhat of all these therein; 'twas a fair purple brown. And if one saw this strange creation of Avalon against the lie of the hair there would be no man wise enough to tell its colour, so manifold and changing were its hues.

The fairy bell   Around its neck was a golden chain, and therefrom hung a bell, which rang so sweet and clear that when it began to chime Tristan forgot his sadness and his sorrow, and the longing for Iseult that lay heavy at his heart. So sweet was the tone of the bell that no man heard it but he straightway forgat all that aforetime had troubled him.

Tristan hearkened, and gazed on this

wondrous marvel; he took note of the dog
and the bell, the changing colours of the
hair, and the sweet sound of the chime;
and it seemed to him that the marvel of
the dog was greater than that of the music
which rang ever in his ears, and banished
all thought of sorrow.

He stretched forth his hand and stroked
the dog, and it seemed to him that he
handled the softest silk, so fine and so
smooth was the hair to his touch. And
the dog neither growled, nor barked, nor
shewed any sign of ill temper, however
one might play with it; nor, as the tale
goes, was it ever seen to eat or to drink.

When the dog was borne away Tristan's
sorrow fell upon him as heavy as before,
and to it was added the thought how he
might by any means win Petit-criu, the
fairy dog, for his lady the queen, that
thereby her sorrow and her longing might
be lessened. Yet he could not see how
this might be brought about, either by
craft or by prayer, for he knew well that
Gilân would not have parted with it for
his life. This desire and longing lay
heavy on his heart, but he gave no out-
ward sign of his thought.

As the history of Tristan's deeds shows us, there was at that time in the land of Wales a giant named Urgan, who had his dwelling by the sea shore. Gilân and his folk were under the lordship of this giant, and must pay him tribute that they might dwell in peace. In these days tidings were brought to the court that Urgan had come, and demanded his tribute of cattle, sheep, and swine.

Herewith Gilân began to tell Tristan how this tribute had been laid upon him by force at the first.

"Now tell me, friend," said Tristan, "if I can help thee in such wise that thou shalt shortly be free of this tribute for all the days of thy life, what wilt thou give me?"

"Of a truth," said Gilân, "I will give thee whatever I possess."

Tristan spake further: "Sir Duke, if thou wilt swear that, then will I on my part promise shortly to free thee for ever from Urgan, or to lose my life in the trial."

"Of a truth, Sir Tristan, I will give thee whatever thou dost desire," said Gilân. "What thou askest, that shall be done," and he gave him his hand upon it.

Then Tristan sent straightway for horses and armour, and bade the folk tell him whither that devil's son, Urgan, would journey with his spoil. Then they shewed him how that the way of the giant lay through a wild wood which bordered on his own lands, and by a bridge over the which he must needs drive the cattle.

The giant came thither with his spoil, but Tristan was before him, and would let the cattle go no further.

When Urgan saw there was a foe on the bridge he came swiftly, with a long steel staff in his hand, which he brandished aloft.

But when he saw the knight so well armed he spake, saying : " Friend on the horse, who art thou? Why dost thou not suffer me and my cattle to pass ? Since thou hast so done thou must die, or yield thee captive."

Then the knight on the horse answered : " Friend, men call me Tristan, know that well; and I fear neither thee nor thy staff a straw ! Turn thee aside, for know surely thy spoil goeth no further."

" Yea," said the giant ; " Sir Tristan, thou vauntest thee of having slain Morolt

of Ireland, with whom thou didst most un-
justly fight, and whom thou didst slay by
thy pride. Nor is it with me as with that
knight of Ireland whom thou didst mock,
and stole from him that fair lady Iseult,
whom he rightly claimed. Nay, nay, this
shore is mine, and I am Urgan ; out of my
path swiftly ! "

Herewith he dealt a sweeping blow at
Tristan, and had taken his aim so well
that had he smitten him he had been slain
forthwith.

Of the   Tristan swerved aside, yet not so swiftly
fight but that the giant's blow fell on the steed
between and cut it in twain.
Tristan
and the   The monster shouted aloud, and cried
giant laughing to Tristan : " God help thee, Sir
Tristan ! Ride not away, but grant me
my prayer, if I may make request unto
thee. Let my tribute pass in peace and
honour ! "

Tristan, seeing his horse was slain, dismounted, and took his spear in his hand,
and smote Urgan with it so that he
wounded him in the eye ; and as the giant
stretched out his hand to take his staff
again, Tristan drew his sword, and smote
off his hand so that it fell to the earth.

Then he smote him another blow on the leg, and drew back. But Urgan seized the staff in his left hand, and ran upon Tristan, and chased him hither and thither under the trees.

But now was the flow of blood from his wound so great that the giant feared his strength would fail him. He left the knight and the cattle, and took up his hand as it lay on the grass, and fled to his fortress.

Tristan stood alone in the wood with the spoil, not a little troubled that Urgan had departed thence alive. He sat him down on the grass, and bethought him what it were best to do. For the regaining of the tribute alone he cared not a jot; if the giant lived he might scarce claim the fulfilment of Gilân's promise. So he turned him about, and followed the blood-stained track which Urgan had left on grass and shrubs. Thus he came to the castle, and entered, and sought Urgan hither and thither, but found neither him nor any living man, for the tale saith that the giant had laid his severed hand on the table in the hall, and gone forth from his castle in the valley to the mountain to seek herbs of healing for his wound. For he knew well their virtue, and that if he could lay the hand to his arm skilfully, ere it grew cold, he should be healed.

But this might not be; for Tristan came thither and spied the hand, and as he found no man there, he took it and bare it away with him.

When Urgan came back, and saw he had lost his hand, he was wrathful indeed, and casting aside the healing herbs, he pursued after Tristan, who had already crossed the bridge, and knew well that the giant was on his track. He took the hand and hid it 'neath the trunk of a tree, and for the first time he began to fear the monster, for he saw well that the matter must be the death of one or other of them. Then he turned him back to the bridge, and met Urgan, and smote him with his spear so fiercely that it brake in two; and as he did so the giant struck at him with his staff. Had the blow fallen on Tristan he must have perished, had he been made of brass; but in his wrath and haste Urgan overreached himself, and the blow fell beyond Tristan, and ere he might draw back his staff Tristan had smitten him in the other eye.

Then Urgan laid around him fiercely on
all sides, as a blind man may, and Tristan
fled from him, and let him deal blows all
around. At last he came within reach,
and the knight put forth all his might, and
with both hands thrust him off the bridge,
so that he fell, and was crushed by his own
weight on the rocks below.

Of the
death of
the giant

Then the victor, Tristan, took the giant's
hand, and fared homewards, and full soon
he met Gilân the duke riding towards him,
for it had grieved him much that Tristan
had taken this venture on himself, for he
had little thought that he might escape as
he had done. When he saw him running
towards him he cried : " Welcome, welcome, gentle Tristan. Say, friend, how is
it with thee ? Art thou whole and un-
wounded ? "

Forthwith Tristan shewed him the dead
hand of the giant, and told him how good
luck had been his portion.

At this Gilân was greatly rejoiced. He
rode straightway to the bridge and saw the
shattered corpse of the giant, even as
Tristan had told him, and marvelled much
at it. Then they returned gaily, driving
the cattle before them ; and the tale went

abroad through all the land of Wales, and
men praised Tristan, so that never more in
that land did men win a third part of the
praise that was sung and spoken of him.

But Tristan and Gilân returned to the
duke's palace; and as they spake of their
good fortune Tristan said: "My lord
duke, I would remind thee of thy promise
and of the oath that was sworn betwixt us
ere I set forth."

And Gilân answered: "That oath will I
keep willingly. Tell me, what dost thou
desire?"

"Duke Gilân, I pray thee, give me the
dog, Petit-criu."

Quoth Gilân: "I would counsel thee
better."

"Let me hear what thou wouldst say."

"Leave me my little dog, and I will
give thee my fair sister, and with her the
half of my kingdom."

"Nay, nay, my lord duke, bethink
thee of thine oath. 'Twas *I* should choose,
and neither land nor riches will I have. I
slew Urgan the giant for nought else but
to win Petit-criu."

"Alas! my lord Tristan, if that be indeed
thy will, I will keep faith with thee and do

thy pleasure. Neither craft nor cunning
am I minded to use. Though it be greatly
against my will, yet what thou desirest that
shall be done."

Herewith he bade them bring the little **Tristan**
dog. "See," he spake, "I will tell thee, **wins the**
and swear to thee on my eternal bliss, that **fairy dog**
I have nothing and may win nothing so
precious (save life and honour) that I
would not rather give thee than this my
dog. Now take him, and God grant it
may be for thy happiness. Thou hast in
truth taken from me the greatest delight of
mine eyes, and much of my heart's joy."

But Tristan was more joyful at having
won the little dog than if Rome and all its
riches, nay, all the kingdoms of the world,
had been his. In comparison with Petit-
criu he held them all not worth a straw.
Never had he been so glad, save when with
Iseult.

Then secretly he called to him a min- **And**
strel of Wales, and counselled him how he **sends it to**
should bring joy to the Queen Iseult. He **Iseult**
hid the little dog cunningly within a lute,
and bade the minstrel bear letters to the
queen, telling her why and by what means
he had won the dog for her.

The minstrel went his way, even as Tristan had commanded, and came without misfortune or ill hap to King Mark's castle at Tintagel. There he sought out Brangœne, and gave letter and dog into her charge, that she might bear them to Iseult. The queen marvelled much at the little dog, and gave the minstrel for reward ten marks of gold. She also wrote a letter that he might bear back to Tristan, telling him that King Mark was well disposed towards him, and had never held him in greater favour than now. She had so managed the matter that he might well return to court.

Tristan did as she prayed him and returned forthwith; king and court, folk and land, held him in honour even as heretofore; never had he been in higher favour, even so much so that both Marjodo and the dwarf Melot must perforce shew him honour—if that may well be said to be honour that cometh not from the heart, but from the lips only.

How the lovers were
banished from court
& dwelt afar in the
forest & how King
Mark was persuaded
of their innocence, &
took his wife again

ow Iseult the queen told her husband that the dog had been sent to her by her mother, the wise Queen of Ireland. She bade them make for it a fair little house, of gold and cunning work, with a rich silk whereon it might lie, and ever, night and day, would she have it in her sight. Wherever she went, whether on horse or afoot, there the dog must be with her. Yet she did this, not for the lessening of her sorrow, but for the love of Tristan who had sent it to her. In sooth no other profit might she have of it, for when the dog was first brought to the queen, and she heard the bell ring softly, and through the sweet chime forgat her grief, she bethought her how her lover Tristan was still weighed down with sorrow for her sake, and she said to herself: "Alas, alas! and shall I be joyful? 'Twere faithless indeed did I rejoice the while *he* sorrows, who hath given over life and happiness to grief and heaviness for my sake! How may I smile when Tristan knoweth no

How Iseult broke off the bell from the neck of Petit-criu

gladness apart from me? He hath nothing
in life save my love. Can I live glad and
joyful while he is sad? God forbid that I
should know happiness apart from him."
Herewith she brake off the bell, leaving
the chain round the dog's neck. But when
the bell was thus broken off it lost all its
magic power; it might ring henceforth, but
never might it bring peace to the heart of
man more. Yet so had Iseult willed it,
that true and faithful lover, apart from
Tristan would she not be joyful, for all
her heart and life had she given unto him.

So were Tristan and Iseult once more
together; once more held in honour by all
the courtiers, and beloved by King Mark;
and once more it behoved them to keep
their secret hidden from all, in so far as
love might do so, for it is but blind—and
was their companion at all times.

But now are the seeds of love and suspicion alike: where they be sown, there
they take root, and bud, and bring forth
fruit; and thus suspicion began ere long to
make sport of Tristan and Iseult—in their
looks and gestures men saw the assurance
of their love. For however lovers may
guard their speech, yet are they gladly in

each other's presence; the eye follows the
heart, the hand the pain.   Thus they built
up suspicion by many a soft glance and
stolen hand-clasp.   And King Mark
watched them closely, and saw their love
written in their faces, though otherwise he
might find but little assurance of it.

Yet their glances were so soft, so sweet, *Of the*
so full of longing, that they went to his *love of*
heart, and such anger awoke therein, such *Tristan*
hatred and envy, that his senses were *and Iseult*
bewildered, and he knew not what to do. *and the*
For the thought that his heart's beloved, *wrath of*
Iseult, should love another better than *King*
himself wrought in him deadly rage. *Mark*
However wrathful he might be, Iseult was
dearer to him than his life, and yet, dearly
as he loved her, he could think of nought
but his anger.   So betwixt the two was
King Mark sore perplexed, till at length,
for very anger, he cared not a jot which
side the truth lay.

Thus blinded by passion, he summoned
them both to the palace court, where all
the courtiers were met together, and he
spoke thus to Iseult : " My Lady Iseult of
Ireland, 'tis well known to all the folk and
the land that for long while, and at many

times, thou hast been under heavy suspicion with my nephew Tristan. Many ways have I tried, openly and in secret, to lead thee for my sake to put aside this folly, yet to no purpose. I am not so foolish nor so besotted but that I can see that openly and secretly thine eyes and thine heart are set upon my nephew. Thou shewest greater kindness to him than to me; by thine actions and bearing I see well that he is dearer to thee than I. No precautions I may take towards thee or towards him may avail; all I do is done in vain. I have separated ye in body so long 'tis a marvel your hearts are yet so at one. Your sweet glances have I severed, yet I may not sever your love. I have borne it too long, herewith will I make an end. The shame and scandal ye have brought upon me will I share with ye no longer. I suffer this dishonour no more from henceforth. Yet will I not revenge myself upon ye, as I well have the right to do. Nephew Tristan, my wife Iseult, that I should put ye two to death, or do ye any hurt, for that do I love ye too well. But now since I see clearly that ye each hold the other dearer than ye do me, so be ye with each other henceforth,

nor have further fear of me. From this
time forward I meddle with ye no more.
Take each other by the hand and leave my
court. If ye wrong me, I will neither see
nor hear it. We three can no longer keep
companionship. I loose me from the bond
and leave ye twain. Such fellowship is ill
—the king who knowingly doth company
with lovers doeth foolishly. Go forth, ye
two, love and live as it shall please ye ; of
our fellowship are ye no more."

Tristan and Iseult are banished from court

'Twas done even as King Mark said.
Tristan and his lady Iseult, cold at heart,
bowed to the king their lord, and to the
courtiers ; then the faithful lovers took
each other by the hand, and passed from
the court. They bade farewell to their
friend Brangœne, and bade her abide at
court till she might hear how matters
went with them. Tristan took twenty
marks of the queen's gold for their needs,
and bade men bring him what he desired
for the journey, harp and sword, crossbow
and horn, and one of his hounds called
Hiudan, which he had chosen from among
the others. He commended his men to
God, and bade them return to their own
land, to Rual his father, save Kurwenal

only, him would he take with him. He
bade him carry the harp, while he himself
took crossbow, horn, and dog (Hiudan, not
Petit-criu). Thus the three rode from
court.

Brangœne abode alone ; the sorrow and
grief of their ill venture and the parting
from her friends went so near to her heart
'twas a marvel she died not of sorrow.
Tristan and Iseult, too, grieved much at
parting from her, yet they hoped that her
wit might find means to make peace once
more betwixt them and King Mark.

They
take their
way to
the
wilder-
ness
So the three rode towards the wilderness,
two days' journey, through woods and over
moorland.

Now, Tristan aforetime knew of a cave
in a wild hill, which he had once chanced
upon while hunting. This same cavern in
the old days of heathendom, when giants
were lords of the land, had been hewn by
them in the hillside. 'Twas there they
were wont to resort secretly for love-
dalliance, and when any such were found
they were shut in with brazen doors and
named Love Grottoes.

The cavern was round, large, and lofty ;
the walls snow-white and smooth ; the vault

above bare in the centre, at the keystone, a crown richly wrought in metal work and adorned with gems; the floor below was of polished marble, its hue green as grass.

In the centre was a couch, carved out of a crystal stone, with letters engraven all around, saying 'twas dedicated to the Goddess of Love. High in the wall of the cavern were little windows hewn in the rock, through which the light might enter. Before the entrance was a brazen door, and without there stood three lindens and no more; but all around the hill and towards the valley were countless trees, whose boughs and foliage gave a fair shade. On one side was a little glade and a spring of water, cool and fresh and clear as sunlight, and above the spring were again three lindens, which sheltered it alike from sun and rain; and all over the glade the bright blossoms and green grass strove with each other for the mastery, each would fain overcome the brightness of the other.

In the branches the birds sang sweetly, so sweetly that nowhere else might one hear the like. Eye and ear alike found solace. There were shade and sunshine, air and soft breezes.

From this hill and this grotto for a good day's journey was there nought but rocks, waste and wild and void of game. Nor was the road smooth and easy, yet was it not so rough but that Tristan and his true love might make their way thither and find shelter in the hill.

Now when they had come to their journey's end, and thought to abide there, they sent Kurwenal back, bidding him say at the court that Tristan and Iseult, with much grief, had sailed thence to Ireland to make their innocence plain to all ; and he had thought it best to return straightway to court. Then they bade him seek out Brangœne and give her tidings of her friends, and learn from her how it stood with King Mark, and if he had lent an ear to evil counsels, and purposed any treachery against the life of the lovers. He was thus to watch how matters went for Tristan and Iseult, and once in every twenty days bear them tidings from the court.

What more shall I say ? Kurwenal did as he was bade, and Tristan and Iseult remained alone to make their dwelling in this wild hermitage.

Many have marvelled wherewith the

twain might support their life in this wilder- Of the
ness, but in truth they needed little save life of the
each other, the true love and faith they bare lovers in
the one to the other, such love as kindles wilder-
the heart and refreshes the soul, that was ness
their best nourishment. They asked but
rarely for other than the food which
giveth to the heart its desire, to the
eyes their delight; therewith had they
enough.

Nor did it vex them that they were thus
alone in the wild woodland; what should
they want with other company? They
were there together, a third would but have
made unequal what was equal, and oppressed
that fellowship which was so fair. Even
good King Arthur never held at his court
a feast that might have brought them
greater joy and refreshment. Search through
all the lands, and ye might not have found
a joy, however great, for which these
twain would have bartered a glass finger
ring.

They had a court, they had a council,
which brought them nought but joy. Their
courtiers were the green trees, the shade
and the sunlight, the streamlet and the
spring; flowers, grass, leaf and blossom,

which refreshed their eyes. Their service
was the song of the birds, the little brown
nightingales, the throstles, and the merles ;
and other wood birds. The siskin and the
ring-dove vied with each other to do them
pleasure ; all day long their music rejoiced
ear and soul.

Their love was their high feast, which
brought them a thousand times daily the joy
of Arthur's Round Table and the fellowship
of his knights. What might they ask
better ? The man was with the woman and
the woman with the man, they had the
fellowship they most desired, and were
where they fain would be.

How   In the dewy morning they gat them
Tristan forth to the meadow where grass and
and Iseult
spent   flowers alike had been refreshed. The
their days glade was their pleasure ground — they
wandered hither and thither, hearkening
each other's speech and waking the song of
the birds by their footsteps. Then they
turned them to where the cold clear spring
rippled forth, and sat beside its stream, and
watched its flow till the sun grew high in
heaven, and they felt its heat. Then they
betook them to the linden : its branches
offered them a welcome shelter, the breezes

were sweet and soft beneath its shade, and the couch at its feet was decked with the fairest grass and flowers.

There they sat side by side, those true lovers, and told each other tales of those who ere their time had suffered and died for love. They mourned the fate of the sad Queen Dido; of Phyllis of Thrace; and Biblis, whose heart brake for love. With such tales did they beguile the time. But when they would think of them no more they turned them again to their grotto and took the harp, and each in their turn sang to it softly lays of love and of longing; now Tristan would strike the harp while Iseult sang the words, then it would be the turn of Iseult to make music while Tristan's voice followed the notes. Full well might it be called the Love Grotto.

At times they would ride forth with the crossbow to shoot the wild game of the woodland, or to chase the red deer with their hound Hiudan, for Tristan had taught him to hunt hart and hind silently, nor to give tongue when on their track. This would they do many days, yet more for the sake of sport and pleasure than to supply themselves with food, for in sooth they had no care save to do what might please them best at the moment.

While they thus dwelt in the woods, King Mark in his palace was but sorrowful, for he grieved ever for his honour and for his wife, and his heart grew heavier day by day.

How King Mark rode forth to the chase In these days, more to solace himself than for love of adventure, he bethought him to ride forth to the chase, and by chance he came into that very wood where Tristan and Iseult had their dwelling. The huntsmen and their dogs came upon a herd of deer and separated a strange stag from among them. He was white, with a mane like to that of a horse, and larger than stags are wont to be. His horns were small and short, scarce grown, as if he had but lately shed them ; and they chased this stag hotly till evening, but he fled from thence to the wood of the Grotto, whence he came, and thus escaped.

King Mark was greatly vexed, and the huntsman even more, that they had lost the quarry (for the beast was passing strange in form and colour), and they were all ill pleased. So they turned not homeward, but encamped in the wood for the night, thinking to take up the chase on the morrow.

Now, Tristan and Iseult had heard all day long the sound of the chase, for the wood rang with the horns and the baying of the hounds. They thought it could be no one but Mark, and their hearts grew heavy within them, for they deemed they were betrayed.

The next morning the chief huntsman arose ere the flush of dawn was in the sky; he bade his underlings wait till the day had fully broken and then follow him. In a leash he took a brachet, which served him well and led him on the right track. It guided him onwards through many rough places, over rocks and hard ground, through barren lands and over grass where yestereven the stag had fled before him. The huntsman followed straight on the track till at last the narrow path came to an end, and the sun shone out clearly; he was by the spring in Tristan's glade.

That same morning had Tristan and his lady love stolen forth, hand in hand, and come full early, through the morning dew, to the flowery meadow and the lovely vale. Dove and nightingale saluted them

sweetly, greeting their friends Tristan and
Iseult. The wild wood birds bade them
welcome in their own tongue,—'twas as if
they had conspired among themselves to
give the lovers a morning greeting. They
sang from the leafy branches in changeful
wise, answering each other in song and
refrain. The spring that charmed their
eye and ear whispered a welcome, even as
did the linden with its rustling leaves.
The blossoming trees, the fair meadow,
the flowers and the green grass, all that
bloomed laughed at their coming ; the dew
which cooled their feet, and refreshed their
heart, offered a silent greeting.

When the twain had rejoiced them
enough in the fair morning air they betook
them again to their grotto, fearing lest the
hunt might come their way, and one of the
hounds discover their hiding-place. After
awhile they laid them down on the couch,
apart, and Tristan laid his unsheathed
sword between them—so they fell asleep.

Now, the huntsman of whom I spake
but now, who had followed the trail of the
stag to the spring, he spied in the morning
dew the track left by Tristan and his lady,
and he bethought him 'twas but the trial

he was following. So he dismounted and followed, till he came to the door of the grotto; 'twas fastened with two bolts, so that he might go no further.

Marvelling much, he turned aside, and sought all around and over the hill, till by chance he found a little window, high up in the wall of the grotto. Fearing greatly he looked through, and saw nought but a man and a woman. Yet the sight moved him to wonder, for he thought that of a truth the woman came of no mortal race, none such had ever been born into this world. Yet he did not stay long at gaze, for he spied the unsheathed sword, and drew back in terror—he deemed that here was magic at work, and was affrighted to remain. So he made his way down the hill and rode back towards the hounds.

The huntsman finds the Love Grotto and beholds the lovers

Now, King Mark had become aware that his chief huntsman had ridden forth after the stag, and had hastened to meet him.

"Sir King," said the huntsman, "I will tell thee a marvel; I have but now found a fair adventure!"

He tells the tale to King Mark

"Say, what adventure?"

"I have found a Love Grotto!"

"Where and how didst thou find it?"

"Sire, here, in this wilderness."

"What? Here, in this wild woodland?"

"Yea, even here."

"Is there any living soul within?"

"Sire, a man and a goddess are within. They lie side by side on a couch and seem to slumber. The man is even as other men, but I doubt me for his companion, if she be mortal! She is more beautiful than a fairy. Never was any so fair of mortal flesh. And between them lieth a sword, bare, bright, and keen. I know not what it may betoken."

The king quoth: "Lead me thither."

The master huntsman led him forthwith on the track of the game to the spot where he had dismounted. The king alighted on the grass, and followed the path the huntsman shewed him. So came King Mark to the door, and turned aside and climbed the hill even to the summit, making many a twist and turn as the huntsman had told him. And he, too, found at last the window and looked through, and saw the twain lie on the crystal couch, sleeping as before; and he saw them even as the huntsman had said, apart, with the naked sword blade between them, and knew them for his nephew and his wife.

His heart grew cold within him for sorrow, and e'en for love, for the strange chance brought him alike grief and joy— joy, from the thought that they were indeed free from guile; sorrow, since he believed what he saw.

And he spake in his heart : " Nay, what may this mean ? Are they indeed guilty as I deemed, then what doeth the sword here ? One would say they are in truth no lovers. Are they verily guilty or not ?" And one while his heart said *Yea* and another while *Nay*.

Then Love, the Reconciler, crept near to King Mark, and laid the golden lie before his eyes, and the *Nay* shone in fair colours into his heart; but the *Yea*, the very truth, it pained him so sore he would not look upon it, for the tempting vision of their golden innocence drew him on to the Easter-day of gladness, where in the light of dawn lay all his joy.

He gazed on his heart's delight, Iseult, and deemed that never before had he seen her so fair. She lay sleeping, with a flush as of mingled roses on her cheek, and her red and glowing lips apart; a little heated by her morning wandering in the dewy meadow and by the spring. On her head was a chaplet woven of clover. A ray of sunlight from the little window fell upon her face, and as Mark looked upon her he longed to kiss her, for never had she seemed so fair and so loveable as now.

He shields Iseult's slumber and goes his way And when he saw how the sunlight fell upon her he feared lest it harm her, or awaken her, so he took grass and leaves and flowers, and covered the window therewith, and spake a blessing on his love and commended her to God, and went his way, weeping.

A sorrowful man, the king returned to the huntsman, and bade him lead his hounds homeward; he would hunt no more in that woodland.

Scarcely had the King departed when Tristan and Iseult awoke from their slumber. Then they looked around them and marvelled to see that the sun shone in but at two windows, and not at three, as it was wont to do. And when they saw the third was darkened they arose with one accord and went out of the grotto, and found the window covered with grass and flowers. Then they looked on the sand before the doorway, and found there the tracks of men's footsteps, and feared greatly lest Mark had been there, and had discovered their hiding-place. They might in no wise be certain, yet it comforted them to think that even if he had seen them, there would have been nought to rouse his anger.

Then King Mark, when he had returned, called his kinsmen and his council toge-ther, and told them what he had found, and said henceforth would he believe nothing against Tristan and Iseult. His lords saw how it stood with the king, and that his desire was to recall the twain, so like wise men they gave counsel according to the desire of the heart, and bade him send messengers to fetch his wife Iseult and his nephew Tristan, since they had done nought against his honour, and he would henceforth believe no evil of them. *King Mark declares the lovers' innocence*

So they sent for Kurwenal, and bade him ride to the woodland and say that the king sent greeting and love to Tristan and the queen, and bade them come again, and none should speak evil of them.

How it fell out that Saint Marie found the lovers sleeping & how they parted the one from the other.

ow King Mark and his courtiers were in all things anxious to do them honour, yet they might no longer be openly friendly as before, for Mark, the doubter, prayed them straitly for God's sake, and for his, to keep a watch on their looks and words, and no longer to shew each other favour and confidence as of yore; and this grieved the lovers sorely.

But King Mark was joyful: he had as much happiness as his heart desired with his lady Iseult; he would that all should shew her open honour, and nothing rejoiced him more than that she should be hailed as queen and lady wherever he was king and lord. 'Tis the blindness of love that will close its eyes to that which it would not see. For in truth he knew that his wife's heart and soul were given to Tristan, yet would he not know it.

To whom then shall the shame or his dishonour be given? For in truth 'twere wrong to say that Tristan and Iseult

Of the folly of King Mark

deceived him; he saw with his eyes, and knew, unseeing, that she loved him not; and yet he loved her!

Alas! many a Mark and many an Iseult doth one see to-day—men who are blind, or whose hearts and eyes are blind. Many are there who hug their blindness, and will not see that which lieth before their eyes, but hold for a lie that which their heart knoweth to be the truth. And would we look upon it fairly, then ought we scarce to blame the woman, if she let the man see that which she doth think and do. For so soon as a man seeth the shame, then is he no longer deceived, but hath at his own will turned his back upon the truth. And in truth the wondrous beauty of Iseult had so fettered King Mark's eyes and senses that he could not see in her aught that should displease him, for he loved her so well that he overlooked all the sorrow she might cause him.

But to Iseult separation from Tristan was even as death; the more her husband forbade her to shew favour and kindness towards him the more her heart clung to him. For this is ever the way of women; children of Mother Eve are they all; 'twas

she who brake the first commandment.
For our Lord God bade her do as she
would with fruit, flowers, and grass, all
that was in the fair garden of Paradise save
one tree only (and the priests say 'twas the
fig-tree), the which was forbidden her on
peril of death. Yet she plucked the fruit,
and brake the commandment, and lost
Paradise.

Now is it my firm belief that Eve would
never have desired to eat of that tree had it
not been forbidden to her. Even so the
first thing that she did shewed of what
mind she was, for 'twas the thing that she
was forbidden. Of every fruit might she
eat at her pleasure, yet would she have
none save that for which she must pay so
heavily.

Yet what greater honour may a woman
have than that she fight against her love
and her desire for the sake of honour?
For in sooth the strife shall end in that her
womanhood and her honour alike be justified; and he who is beloved of such a lady
findeth himself elect to all bliss. He hath
Paradise in his heart, and need vex himself
with no fear lest the serpent be hidden
amongst the flowers, or that a thorn will

pierce his hand if he pluck a rose, for thorns and thistles alike are banished from that garden.

But alas! such happiness was not for Tristan and Iseult; the watch they must keep upon their words and looks was bitter to them both, and never had they sought so earnestly for means whereby they might come together; yet when they found them 'twas but to their sorrow and bitter grief.

The last meeting of Tristan and Iseult It was midday, and the sun shone hotly, so that the queen would no longer abide in the palace, but took her way forth to the orchard. There, under the cool shade of a tree, she bade her maidens prepare a couch that she might rest awhile. This they did, spreading the couch with purple and fine linen, and Queen Iseult bade them leave her, all save Brangœne alone.

Then, since the place was lonely, and none were abroad at that hour, she sent Brangœne secretly to Tristan, bidding him come and speak with her. This she did, and Tristan did even as Adam when Eve proffered him the fruit—he took it, and ate death thereof with her.

But Brangœne went away sadly, bidding the chamberlain see that none enter the

queen's apartments, and sat herself down
by one of the doors, sorrowing to think
that her caution and her counsel might not
serve her lady better.

Scarcely had the chamberlain taken his
stand before the door ere King Mark came
towards him, and asked impatiently for the
queen.

"She sleepeth, sire," answered her
maidens; and Brangœne, as she sat, hid
her face in her hands, for her heart failed
her.

But the King said: "Where doth the
queen sleep?" And they told him, in the
garden. And Mark went thither and
found his heart-sorrow, for there lay his
wife and his nephew, clasped in each other's
arms, cheek to cheek, and lip to lip. So
were Mark's doubts at an end—he suspected no more, for he knew.

*King
Mark
discovers
the lovers
and
learns the
truth*

Silently he turned and went his way,
and calling the lords of his council, told
them how Tristan and the queen were
even now together, and bade them go, and
take the twain, and judge them according
to the law of the land.

But even as Mark turned to go Tristan
awoke, and saw him, and said within him-

self: "Alas! what hast thou done, faithful Brangœne? I wot well this shall be our death! Awake, Iseult, unhappy love, heart's queen, we are betrayed!"

"Betrayed?" she spake, "how may that be?"

The fare-
well of
the lovers "My lord the king stood but now above us; he saw us, and I saw him. Now hath he gone to bring witnesses, he worketh for our death. Heart's lady, fair Iseult, now must we part, never again may we rejoice in each other as aforetime. Now bethink thee of the true love that hath been betwixt us, and see that it remain ever steadfast, let me not out of thine heart! For whatever befall mine, thou shalt never depart from it. Iseult must ever dwell in Tristan's heart! See, love, that neither time nor distance change thy mind towards me. Forget me not, whatever befall. Sweet love, fair Iseult, kiss me, and bid me farewell!"

She stepped a little back, and spake, sighing: "Our hearts and our souls have been too long and too closely knit together that they may ever learn forgetfulness. Whether thou art far or near, in my heart shall be nothing living save Tristan alone

—my love and my life. Body and soul
have been thine this long while ; see that
no other woman ever separate thee from
me, so that our love and our faith be not
ever steadfast and true as they have been
betwixt us these many years. And take
thou this ring, let it be a token to thee of
faith and love, that at any time if thou
lovest other than me thou mayest look
upon it and remember how thou abidest in
mine heart. Think of this parting, how
near it goeth to heart and life ! Remember
the many heavy sorrows I have suffered
through thee, and let none be ever nearer
to thee than Iseult ! Forget me not for
the sake of another ! We two have loved
and sorrowed in such true fellowship unto
this time, we should not find it over-hard to
keep the same faith even to death. Yet
methinks 'tis needless to remind thee thus.
If Iseult were ever one heart and one faith
with Tristan, that is she now, that must
she ever be. Yet would I fain make one
prayer to thee : whatever land thou seekest,
have a care for thyself—*my* life ; for if I be
robbed of that, then am I, *thy* life, undone.
And myself, *thy* life, will I for thy sake,
not for mine, guard with all care. For

thy body and thy life, that know I well,
they rest on me. Now bethink thee well
of me, thy body, Iseult. Let me see my
life in thee, if it may well be so, and see
thou thy life in me! Thou guardest the
life of both. Now come hither and kiss
me. Tristan and Iseult, thou and I, we
twain are but one being, without distinc-
tion or difference. This kiss shall be a
seal that I thine, and thou mine, remain
even to death but one Tristan and one
Iseult!"

How Tristan departed from Iseult Now that they had set the seal on their
covenant, Tristan departed thence, with
bitter sorrow; his self, his other life, Iseult,
remained weeping sorely. Never aforetime
had their parting been thus sorrowful.

Herewith came the king, and with him
a company of his lords and counsellors, yet
they came too late, for they found but
Iseult alone.

Then they drew the king aside, and
said : "Sire, herein hast thou wronged both
thy wife and thine honour. Now, as many
a time before, hast thou accused the queen
needlessly and for nought. Thou wrongest
thyself. How canst thou be joyful the
while thou dost shame thy wife, and make

her and thyself the mock of the land?
Yet hast thou found no wrong in her.
Why slander the queen who hath not betrayed thee? For thine own self and
thine honour do so no more." Thus they
counselled him; and Mark held his peace,
and went thence unavenged.

Herein ye may read the ending of Tristan & Iseult ❦ Of Tristan's valiant deeds ❦ How he wedded Iseult of the white hands ❦ Of his deadly wound ❦ Of the coming of Iseult of Ireland & of the death of the lovers.

RISTAN betook him to his lodging, and bade his folk make ready and come with him swiftly to the haven. There he went aboard the first ship he found, and sailed with his men to Normandy. But there he abode not long, for he sought a life that should bring him some comfort for his sadness. He fled from death that he might seek death, and so free him from the death of the heart—his separation from Iseult. What profit to flee from death if he bare death with him ? What profit if the torment that drave him forth from Cornwall yet lay, day and night, upon him ?

He bethought him that if his sorrow were ever to be lessened it must needs be by deeds of knighthood ; so hearing that there was war in Almayne, he journeyed thither, and served sceptre and crown so faithfully that the Roman Empire never won under its banners a warrior who wrought such mighty deeds. Many an adventure had he, the which I will not

recount, for if I were to tell all the deeds
that have been written of him, the tale
would indeed be marvellous! But the
many fables men tell of him I cast to the
winds; 'tis toil and labour enow to record
the truth.

Tristan's life and death, the fair-haired
Iseult, she had sorrow and grief enough.
Her heart well nigh broke as she watched
his ship sail thence; but his life kept her in
life—apart from him she might neither live
nor die. She watched the sail flutter in
the wind, and spake in her heart: "Alas,
alas! Sir Tristan, my heart clingeth to thee,
my eyes follow thee, and thou speedest
from me! Why go thus quickly?
Knowest thou not that thou dost flee thy
life in fleeing from Iseult? Thou canst
no more live a day without me than I can
live without thee. Our lives are so inter-
woven that thou bearest my life with thee;
and though in sooth thou leavest thine, yet
may neither of us rightly die nor fully live!
So am I, poor Iseult, henceforth neither
dead nor living! What may I do, alas?
I am here, and I am there, yet am I in
neither place. I see myself on the sea,
and know myself on the land. I sail hence

*How
Iseult
made
lamenta-
tion*

with Tristan, and sit here beside King
Mark!" So she bemoaned herself.

When Tristan had been half a year and
more in Almayne he became heavy at
heart, hearing nought of his lady, and
thought to return to the land where he
might hear some rumours of her doings.
So he gat him back to Normandy, and
from thence to Parmenie, thinking that he
would find comfort and counsel with Rual.
But alas! he and his wife were both dead,
yet his sons welcomed Tristan gladly, and
were joyful at his coming. They kissed
his hands and feet, eyes and mouth, many
a time. "Lord," they said, "in thee hath
God given us back both father and mother.
Now abide here with us, and take again all
that was thine, and let us serve thee even
as our father served thee, who was thy
man, as we would gladly be! Our father
and mother are alike dead, but God hath
looked upon our need, and sent thee back
to us!"

Then they shewed Tristan the tomb,
and he stood and wept awhile beside it, and
said: "Now if faith and honour may be
buried in the earth, here do they lie en-
tombed. Yet if faith and honour are aught

akin to God, as men say, then doubt I not that these twain are now crowned above, even as the children of God are crowned."

The sons of Rual, even as their father, laid themselves and all they had at Tristan's service, and vexed themselves in all things to do his will ; and thus he abode with them many days.

Now was there a dukedom, betwixt Brittany and England, which was called Arundel, and lay upon the sea coast. The ruler of the land was an old man, but a brave and courteous. The story saith that his neighbours had made war upon him, and had robbed him of possessions by sea and land. Right willingly had he avenged himself, but as yet he lacked the power to do so. One son and one daughter had the duke. The son had received knighthood three years past, and had won much praise and honour for his valiant deeds. His sister was a fair maiden, Iseult of the white hand was she called, and her brother's name was Kahedîn. The duke's name was Jovelîn.

A rumour came to Parmenie that there was fighting in the dukedom of Arundel, and Tristan, thinking thereby to forget

his sorrow, journeyed thither, and found
the duke in his castle of Karke. Thither
went he with all his friends, and the duke
received him with the welcome befitting a
noble warrior, for he knew Tristan well by
report—all the islands of the Western Sea
were full of his fame. The duke was
joyful of his coming, and Kahedîn, his son,
was minded to show him all the honour he
might, and would ever be in his company.
Friendship was sworn betwixt the two,
and they kept that oath faithfully, even
unto their death.

Tristan bade the duke tell him how
matters stood with him ; what was the
might of his enemies, and where they most
straitly beset his land ; and when he knew
that they had in truth a mighty force
against them, he sent secretly to Parmenie,
to Rual's sons, telling them he was in need
of aid ; and they came swiftly, with five
hundred men, and great store of food and
drink, for the duke's foemen had laid the
land waste.

When Tristan knew of their coming he
went to meet them, and led them under
cover of night into the land. One half he
bade abide at the castle of Karke, and keep

their presence secret till he and Kahedîn had need of them. With the other half he rode to a castle which the duke had bidden him guard, and commanded them to lie hidden, even as those at Karke.

Tristan defeats the duke's foes and wins back the land

With the daylight Tristan and Kahedîn rode to the border, burning and sacking every fortress on their path, so that the cry went abroad through all the land that Kahedîn had ridden forth openly to dare the enemy. And when the former heard this they gathered their men together and came out to meet them, and fell in with them beneath the walls of Karke. When the battle was at its height Tristan's knights who had lain hidden within the castle fell upon them suddenly, and thus taken by surprise, the foe could do nought but fly, or yield themselves prisoners, or die on the field.

When they had thus taken the leaders captive, Tristan and Kahedîn, with all their knights, rode into the enemy's land. There was no fortress so strong that it might resist them, and all the goods and all the prisoners they won they sent to Karke, till the land was once more in their power, and the duke was well avenged.

Then Tristan bade Rual's sons return to Parmenie, and thanked them much for the aid they had given him. The prisoners he bade receive their lands again from the hands of Duke Jovelîn, and swear to remain his men, and abstain henceforth from making war upon him; and to this all the princes agreed. Hereafter was Tristan held in great honour at court and through all the land, and all men alike were fain to do his bidding.

Now Kahedîn's sister, Iseult of the white hand, was a fair and noble maiden, the flower of the land for beauty and virtue. As Tristan beheld her the old sorrow awoke in his heart. She reminded him of the other Iseult, the Princess of Ireland; nor might he hear or speak her name but that his sorrow might be read in his face. Yet he loved the grief that lay at his heart, and saw the maiden gladly, in that she called to his mind the faith he had sworn to the fair-haired Iseult. Iseult was alike his sorrow and his joy; she brought him comfort, and she vexed him sore. The more his heart yearned for the one Iseult, the more gladly he beheld the other.

And he said in his heart: "Yea, God,

Of Iseult of the white hand

Tristan is grieved at heart and sore perplexed how the name doth lead me astray! truth and falsehood betray alike mine eyes and my soul. *Iseult* rings laughing in mine ear at all times, yet know I not who Iseult may be—mine eyes behold her, and yet they see her not. Iseult is far from me, and yet is she near. Once more am I bewitched, and Cornwall hath become Arundel; Tintagel, Karke; and Iseult hath taken the form of Iseult! I deemed when men spake of this maiden as *Iseult*, that I had found my love again—and yet was I deceived. Over-long do I desire the sight of Iseult; now am I come where Iseult is, and find her not! I see her day by day, yet see her not, therefore make I my moan. I have found Iseult, yet not the fair-haired Iseult, who was so kindly cruel. The Iseult who vexeth thus my heart is she of Arundel, not Iseult the fair; she, alas! mine eyes behold not. And yet she whom I now behold, and who is sealed with her name, her I must ever honour and love, for the sake of the dear name that so oft hath given me joy and gladness unspeakable."

So Tristan spake oft with himself, and the maid, Iseult of the white hand, marked

his troubled glances, and saw how they
rested upon her, and her heart went out
towards him, for she heard how throughout
the land all men praised him; and her eyes
strove to answer the thought in him, till
the man began to marvel in his heart
whether here he might not find an ending
to his woe.

Then he upbraided himself for falsehood.
"Ah, faithless Tristan! wouldst thou love
two Iseults, when thine other life, Iseult,
will have but one Tristan? She will have
none other love but me; shall I woo
another? Woe to thee, Tristan, lay aside
this blind folly, and put the thought far from
thee."

So was his heart turned again to the love
that was his true heritage, and he thought
but of his old grief.

Yet was he ever courteous to the maiden
Iseult, and whatever her pleasure might be,
that would he do. He told her knightly
tales, he sang for her, and wrote and read,
even as she bade him. And in those days
he made the noble "Lay of Tristan,"
which men in all lands love and prize, and
shall prize while the world endures. For
often it chanced when all the folk sat to-

gether, Tristan, Iseult, and Kahedîn, the
duke and the duchess, with all the lords
and ladies of the court, that he wove fair
verses, and roundels, and courteous songs,
and ever he sang this refrain:

"Iseut ma drue, Iseut m'amie,
　En vous ma mort, en vous ma vie!"

How
Iseult of
the white
hand
loved
Tristan

But since he was so fain to sing thus, all
who hearkened deemed that he meant their
lady, the maiden Iseult, and were beyond
measure joyful. And none more than
Kahedîn. Many a time and oft did he set
Tristan beside his sister, and she, when
she smiled on Tristan, and gave him her
hand, did it as if to pleasure her brother—
yet was it to pleasure herself.

Yet day by day Tristan's sorrow grew
heavier; he desired but one Iseult, Iseult
of Ireland; and Iseult of the white hand,
she would have none but Tristan. Her
heart and soul were his, his grief was hers,
and as she saw him grow pale and sigh for
sorrow, so she herself sighed and grew
pale, till at length she shewed her love to
him so openly, in sweet gestures, looks, and
words, that he scarce knew what he might
do, and his heart was tossed on a sea of doubt.

And as time passed on, and never word or message came from Queen Iseult, he began to think whether his sorrow and his faith were not all in vain.

"Ah, sweet friend, love Iseult!" he said, "now is our life too far apart. 'Tis no longer as erewhile, when we had but one joy, one sorrow, one love, and one life between us. Now is our fate unlike. I am sad, and thou art joyful. My heart yearneth for thy love, but thy longings for me, they are methinks but feeble. Alas! alas! that which I have lost for thee dost thou hold; thou art at home with thy lord Mark, and thy friends around thee, and I am alone, a stranger in a strange land. Little comfort may I have henceforth from thee, and yet my heart clingeth to thee. Little need hast thou of me! Why dost thou ask not what befalls me? Ah! sweet Queen Iseult, hadst thou departed from me as I from thee, surely had I sent to learn tidings of her who was my life. And yet it may be that she hath sought me, and found me not, for he who seeketh a wanderer hath no fixed goal for his search. She may well have sought secretly through Cornwall and England, through France

How Tristan deemed that Iseult loved him no more

and Normandy, even to my land of Parmenie, and finding me not, she thinketh of
me no more."*

Thus his doubt of Iseult of Ireland, and
the love shewn him by Iseult of the white
hand, wrought on Tristan's heart, and
vexed him day and night, till at last, for
the friendship he bare to Kahedîn, and for
the sweetness and beauty of Iseult the
maiden, he determined to wed her. So the
duke proclaimed a great feast, and the
folk came from far and wide, and Iseult of
the white hand and Tristan were made
man and wife by the bishop of the land, in
the Minster at Karke. And yet, for the
love which he bare to Iseult of Ireland,
which might not be stilled, was she but his
wife in name. Yet none but they two
knew of it, and Iseult's doubts were laid at
rest, for Tristan told her how he had made
a vow, many a year agone, should he ever
wed, to leave his wife a maiden for a
year.

How
Tristan
wedded
Iseult of
the white
hand

Now Kahedîn, Iseult's brother, had
loved, from his youth up, a lady of the
land, and she, too, loved him well; yet her
parents, against her will, had given her in

* End of Gottfried's poem.

marriage to another knight, the lord of Gamaroch, which lay near to the land of Arundel. And there, in his castle of Gamaroch, did her husband keep her strictly guarded, for he knew well that she loved him not; nor would he go abroad save that he bare the keys of the castle with him.

Then Kahedîn in his sorrow took counsel with Tristan, and Tristan bade him, if he could by any means win speech with his lady from without, to pray her to make moulds in wax of the keys while her husband slept, and throw the moulds into the moated ditch below the castle wall. This she did, and with the aid of a cunning smith they made keys that would fit the locks.

Of Kahedin's love adventure and its evil end

So when next Nampotenis, for so was the knight called, rode abroad, and left his wife in guard, Kahedîn and Tristan came secretly, and unlocked the castle gates, and entered. The lady received them with much joy; but as they crossed the moat the wind loosened the circlet from Kahedîn's helmet and it fell to the ground; but neither of the twain were ware of it.

Then Kahedîn and his lady spake together through the hours of the night, and Tristan kept watch without till the dawning. With the morning light they rode away, and deemed that none knew of their coming.

But when Nampotenis came again in the morning, he beheld in the moat the circlet that had fallen from Kahedîn's helmet, and knew well it was none of his or of his knights', and deemed that forsooth his wife's lover had been with her. Then with stern words he bade her confess the truth, and because she greatly feared his wrath and cruelty she told him all; and Nampotenis forthwith called his men together, and pursued after the two knights, and overtook them in the forest.

They had no thought that they were pursued, and were taken at unawares, and ere they wist their foes were upon them Nampotenis fell on Kahedîn and ran him through the body with his spear, so that he fell dead. But Tristan in wrath drew out his sword and ran upon Nampotenis and smote him dead, and put all his men to flight. Yet ere they fled had one of them smitten Tristan through the thigh with a poisoned spear. With great sorrow did Tristan bear his dead comrade back to Karke, and they buried him in the minster.

Iseult of the white hand dressed Tristan's wound, and bade the leeches of the land do what they might to heal him, but nought that they might do was of any avail, for the venom was so potent their skill might not prevail against it.

Of Tristan's deadly wound, and how he sent for Iseult the queen to heal him

Then Tristan saw well how it stood with him, and he said to himself: " Now might I but send to my lady Iseult, methinks she would cure me now, even as her mother did aforetime, otherwise must I die of this hurt." Then secretly he sent for Kurwenal, and prayed him to go with all speed to Tintagel and seek out Iseult the queen. "Bear with thee this ring, and shew it to her as a token from me, and say how that I lie sorely wounded, and must needs die an she come not to mine aid. And if for love of me she will come, then I pray thee to set a white sail to the ship ; but if she cometh not, then let the sail be black, for I shall know she loveth me no more."

Then Kurwenal departed, even as Tristan bade him, and came to Tintagel, and told Iseult the queen secretly all that

Tristan had bade him say. She made ready in haste, and wrapped her in her veil, and stole to the harbour, and sailed away ere any might know of it.

Now Tristan bade them bear him day by day to the shore that he might watch for the ship from Cornwall till his weakness grew so great he might do so no longer; then he bade his wife, Iseult, watch from the window of his chamber and bear him tidings when Kurwenal should return.

But Iseult of the white hand had hearkened secretly when her husband spake to Kurwenal, and her heart was hot within her for anger 'gainst the other Iseult, for she knew well who it was that Tristan loved. So when at last she spied the ship that bare Iseult the queen thither, she said to her husband: "Yonder cometh the ship wherein Kurwenal sailed hence."

"What manner of sail doth it bear?" spake Tristan.

"'Tis black as night," answered Iseult of the white hand, yet she lied, for the sail was white as snow.

Then Tristan spake no word, but turned his face to the wall, and said in his heart: "God keep thee, my love Iseult, for I shall look on thee no more," and with that he loosed his hold of the life he had held till then, and his soul departed.

Now the ship wherein was Iseult of Ireland drew nigh to the haven; and as they came to shore they heard the bells toll from the Minster and the chapels, and the voice of weeping and lamentation in the streets. "What meaneth this woe?" asked Iseult the queen, "and wherefore do ye toll the bells?" Then an old man answered, and said: "Fair lady, a great misfortune hath befallen our land. Tristan, the bravest of knights, he who drave out our enemies and restored our duke to his own, is but now dead. He hath died of a wound from a poisoned spear; but now have they borne his body to the Minster."

Then Iseult answered no word, but turned her on the way to the Minster, and went thither swiftly; and all looked upon her, and marvelled at her beauty and her woe. And when she came to the Minster Tristan lay dead on the bier, and beside him sat Iseult of the white hand. Then Iseult of Ireland looked upon her: "Why sittest thou here beside the dead, thou who hast slain him? Arise, and get thee hence!"

And how she herself departed this life And Iseult of the white hand arose and drew aside, for she feared the queen.

But Iseult of Ireland spake no word more, but laid her down on the bier by her lover, and put her arms around him, and sighed once, and her soul departed from her body.

Now tidings had been brought to King Mark how that Iseult the queen had fled with Kurwenal, and he took ship and pursued after her swiftly, but ere he came to shore at Arundel she lay dead beside Tristan. How King Mark learnt the truth and of the burial of Tristan and Iseult And there Kurwenal told Mark all that had chanced, and the secret of the love potion, and how it was by no will of their own but through the magic of the love drink that the twain had wronged him. And Mark spake, weeping: "Alas! Tristan, hadst thou but trusted in me, and told me all the truth, then had I given Iseult to thee for wife."

Then he bade them embalm the bodies, and he bare them back with him to Tintagel, and laid them in marble tombs on either side of the chapel wherein the kings of his line lay buried. And by the tomb of Tristan he bade them plant a rose-tree, and by that of Iseult a vine, and the two reached towards each other across the chapel, and wove branches and root so closely together that no man hereafter might separate them.

Explicit "Tristan and Iseult."

Notes

PAGE 3.—*The love potion.* There is no doubt that the early tellers of this story had a firm belief in the fatal power of the love potion, and practically regarded the lovers as blameless. This queen-mother, with her skill in spells and potions, recalls the queen-mother of the Volsunga Saga. It has been suggested that this mother and daughter, bearing the same name and alike skilled in healing, show traces of the influence of Northern legend. It will be remembered that Grimhild, the name of the *mother* in the Volsunga Saga, is in the Nibelungen-Lied the name of the *daughter*.

PAGE 27.—*Brangœne's parable.* In the prose versions Brangœne speaks of a lily, not of a white robe. The version in the poem is evidently the more primitive as it is the more dramatic.

PAGE 33.—*Gandin.* The story of the abduction of Iseult by the knight of Ireland may be compared with Hartmann von Aue's version of the *Charrette* adventure, where he represents Meleagaunt as gaining possession of Guinevere by a similar ruse. In Crestien's poem this feature of the rôle is assigned to Kay. In each case the queen is rescued not by her husband but by her lover.

PAGE 59.—"*Take the twig of an olive.*" In some of the versions the stream flows *through* and not past the queen's chamber, thus indicating, as M. Gaston Paris points out, a very primitive state of society and culture. The incident of the snare laid for the lovers appears to be part of the original story, and to have enjoyed considerable popularity. Several pictured representations of this scene have been preserved, principally in the form of stone or ivory carvings.

PAGE 75.—Here occurs an incident which I have omitted in the translation, where Mark is led to suspect the lovers by the traces of blood on the bed-clothes. This may be paralleled by the well-known episode of the *Charrette* poem, where Launcelot, wounding his hands with the bars of the queen's window, brings suspicion alike on Guinevere and on Kay. A similar episode slightly differing in form occurs in the prose *Tristan*. Not all Gottfried's skill could make this incident other than unpoetical and distasteful to modern readers.

PAGE 84.—*The ordeal.* The episode of the ordeal and Iseult's successful ruse is evidently of late introduction. Professor Golther (*Die Sage von Tristan und Isolde*, p. 13) gives a list of variants of this story, drawn from widely different sources, and traces it ultimately to India. As I have noted above, the original tellers of the story really regarded Tristan and Iseult as irresponsible victims of Fate, and evidently saw no incongruity in their appeals to heaven to demonstrate their innocence. Gottfried was far too shrewd (and too modern) really to share this view, though he reproduces it faithfully ; but the issue of the ordeal is evidently a little too much for him, and he indulges in most sarcastic remarks as to the manner in which the Deity may be duped, and become the accomplice of sinners. These remarks I have slightly modified.

PAGE 90.—*Petit-crin.* With this description of the fairy dog from Avalon may be compared that of the hound in *Sir Libeaus Desconus*, which was " as many coloured as the flowers that blossom betwixt May and Midsummer " ; also the brachet in the pursuit of which Schionatulander met his death; (*Titure*) and the horse given by Guivret le Petit to Erec in the poem of that name.

PAGE 107.—*The banishment of the lovers.* This poetical episode, so charmingly described by Gottfried, evidently formed part of the original story. As we see by the poet's remarks (p. 110), the state of society therein pictured was more primitive and Arcadian than that of his day. In the prose *Tristan* we are told that the lovers find a *maison* constructed by a knight of Cornwall for his lady, who was versed in magic, and could by her spells make the dwelling invisible to all save they two alone. Professor Golther sees in this a hint of the origin of Gottfried's Love-Grotto, but I should rather be inclined to detect the influence of the *Merlin* legend, and to assign the Grotto to the *Venus* story. It was surely to some such dwelling that the goddess invited Tannhäuser? Gottfried gives a lengthy and mystical interpretation of the details of the Grotto; this I have omitted. It introduces a discordant note into the simplicity of the story, which belongs to an earlier date than the artificial elaboration of Gottfried's love symbolism.

PAGE 111.—*King Arthur.* This, and the passage on the following page, are the only allusions to Arthurian romance found in the poem. None of the heroes of Arthur's court are mentioned throughout.

PAGE 130.—*The parting of Tristan and Iseult.* In the different continuations of Gottfried's poem, and also in the other versions of the story, the lovers meet more than once after this, Tristan returning to Tintagel in various disguises; but it is difficult to determine whether these incidents really belong to the genuine story or not. There may have been *one* meeting, but it seems probable that several of those related are but variants of one original episode. So far as Gottfried is concerned I find it difficult to believe that he would have weakened the effect of this powerful and pathetic parting by bringing the lovers together again in life. As he recounts no such meeting

I have thought myself justified in passing at once from the conclusion of his poem to the closing scenes.

PAGE 153.—*The meeting of the two Iseults.* This dramatic incident appears only to be preserved by Ulrich von Türheim. It may be a later introduction, due to the *Siegfried* tradition, but it appears to me fine enough to be recorded, and I have therefore introduced it here, though otherwise I have not followed Ulrich's version.